Kathy Santo's Dog Sense

Kathy Santo's Dog Sense

Kathy Santo

Alfred A. Knopf, New York, 2005

THIS IS A BORZOI BOOK
PUBLISHED BY ALFRED A. KNOPF

Copyright © 2005 by Kathy Santo

www.aaknopf.com

Knopf, Borzoi Books, and the colophon are registered
trademarks of Random House, Inc.

Library of Congress Cataloging-in-Publication Data
Santo, Kathy, [date].
    [Dog sense]
    Kathy Santo's dog sense.—1st ed.
        p. cm.
    ISBN 1-4000-4343-3
  1. Dogs—Training.   I. Title: Dog sense.   II. Title.
SF431.S26 2005
636.7'0887—dc22   2004063323

Printed in the United States of America
First Edition

Contents

All of the information in this book is offered under the assumption that your dog is physically healthy and pain free. If you have any doubts, you should see your veterinarian for a complete physical, including blood work to rule out illnesses that might be affecting your dog's behavior.

Introduction

Failure Is Not an Option

"My dog doesn't listen!"; "My dog chews my shoes"; "My dog jumps on people"; "My dog thinks he's walking *me*!"

These are just a few of the complaints I've heard countless times in twenty years of training dogs. People from all walks of life, with dogs of all temperaments, shapes, ages, and breeds, come to me—sometimes in tears—asking for help. I take the leash an owner hands me and look at the dog at the end of it. Usually the dog is jumping, sniffing, or just looking around—lost in a world of his own. He has heard human voices of all kinds, male or female, soft or loud, stern or cajoling. But no matter what kind he has been hearing, the dog has learned to tune them out. He may love or fear his humans, but in most cases he simply ignores them. Here is where I come in.

My stock-in-trade is a knack for connecting with dogs quickly. It seems I've always been able to spend an hour with a dog-and-human pair and figure out what makes their relationship tick. If it's broken, I can fix it.

Over the years I have noticed that my mainly intuitive approach has been, with each dog, both the same and different in interesting ways. Sometimes two dogs with practically the same behavior problem would require very different training strategies. But sometimes basically the same strategy would work for two dogs with very different problems. Among entirely untrained dogs (usually but not always puppies), another interesting pattern appeared: People I had taught to train a first dog would bring me their second and say that they had tried to follow what I had shown them before but this time it hadn't worked—even though the new dog was of the same breed as the previous one. Like the owners, I was at first ready to blame the problem on their lack of the "professional touch." Flattering (to me), maybe, and good for business, but actually untrue, I finally realized.

It took me some time really to understand just what goes on when I work with a dog and an owner. Initially, the process seems too chaotic for words: Dozens of ideas go through my head, though I might speak of only a handful, even if just to myself. In this rapid-fire diagnostic procedure, lots of scenarios and approaches play out mentally, but in practice I always manage to home in on the right one in just a few attempts.

How do I do it?

Partly by assessing the clients first: I listen, find out what's going on in their lives, study their body language—all with an eye for seeing how they relate to their dog. Badly trained dogs often belong to people with habits that have the unintended effect of promoting bad behavior. Speaking in high-pitched babble is one of the most common (and annoying) ways humans unwittingly inspire their dogs to misbehave. But even those with more dulcet voices are frequently led by faulty instinct to make fateful mistakes (for instance, hollering "NOOOO!" when the dog is actually doing precisely what you asked but not what you wanted). Discovering your own misconceptions about how dogs think and recognizing the faux pas in how you handle your four-footed friend can go a long way toward improving his behavior.

But even more important than understanding the client is understanding the dog. If I have a professional secret, it is my awareness that dogs are "people," too. I don't mean this in a cute way. What most humans don't realize when their dog-training efforts fail is that dogs differ dramatically in nature from one individual to another. Consequently, any form of instruction not grounded in a sense of the dog's individuality has a very low probability of success. Conversely, a method customized to meet the dog's specific needs, motivations, and confidence level can be amazingly efficient. In fact, following a training strategy geared to the individual can be so rewarding (for both of you) that your dog can continue to learn and to improve his behavior indefinitely. This insight, more than any "dog whisperer's" gift, has been the secret to my success.

Even a laser-guided system of dog training does take time. A truly well-trained dog requires weeks of active instruction, with clearly communicated and consistently reinforced guidance. Fortunately, even the busiest people realize that an untrained dog can cost them much more than fifteen minutes a day: There is a potentially huge toll in damaged property, lost sleep, and painful effort expended forcing the dog to do what a trained one would do without fuss. And so most are prepared to put in some time to teach the dog acceptable manners—they just don't know how to go about it effectively. Poorly trained dogs are rarely the result of their owners' lack of will; much more likely, the matter is one of misguided effort.

The problem comes when the common "one-size-fits-all" prescriptions for training don't work, or work only partially. Training becomes a chore, and a frustrating one. For this reason, in the majority of cases, active instruction in the dog's life is confined to a training period during which he learns whatever he will learn. Thereafter, typically for the rest of his days, his behavioral traits—good, bad, and ugly—if not completely intolerable are simply accepted as a given, and you learn to work around them. I'm often amazed that a nation with so many ambitions for their houses, their bodies, and their children's sports should have such unnecessarily low expectations of their dogs.

My philosophy holds that any dog can be taught good behavior. And learning can and should continue throughout his life. But such an ambition wouldn't even be conceivable unless the training were not only effective but enjoyable.

You *can* teach an old dog new tricks. In fact, you can—and should—teach a dog of virtually any age. Why? Most urgently for his own safety: A dog who isn't trained is a danger to himself in most settings where people live. But beyond life-and-death matters, there is also quality of life: The more a dog learns, the easier learning becomes, the better his adjustment and conformity to your life, and the stronger your mutual understanding and emotional bond. What's not to love?

I've found that most other training approaches—*some* of them extremely effective with *some* dogs—produce two possible outcomes: success and failure. Unfortunately, the two occur with roughly the same frequency. A "trick" either does the trick or it doesn't. With my approach, failure is simply not an option; it's a prompt to the next possibility. The untrained or "problem" dog is a puzzle for which there is almost always a solution. It's not an ailment for which "the cure" may or may not work.

More than in the average business, in my line of work success depends on clear and fast results. As a dog trainer you can't last for long on hype. In literally thousands of cases, my finished product has been nothing less than a well-balanced team of dog and human, a partnership based on two-way respect and understanding. Still, teaching this system in person is one thing, and articulating it in a book is another. I wouldn't have imagined a book using my interactive approach was possible if it hadn't been for my Web site, www .kathysanto.com. Thanks to some thousand hits a week, I've been forced to put into words the solution to thousands of problems. Answering the questions of people I've never met about dogs I've never seen has shown me that what had seemed "complicated and intuitive" is really quite simple and methodical. I realized that what I do could not only be described but pretty easily learned. Fortunately, this discovery came at roughly the point when the number of prospective clients got beyond what any one person could handle. (I now see one hundred dogs a week and have over one thousand clients in total! And that isn't counting my graduates!)

My aim is to show how you can thoroughly train your own dog. Unlike most training methods, mine is interactive and won't leave you throwing up your hands in despair. Following a course of directed trial and error, you can quickly arrive at a teaching strategy suited to your dog as an individual. With each attempt, effective or ineffective, you will learn something about how your dog learns, something you can use when teaching him next time.

The foundation of all success will be an accurate assessment of the key aspects of your dog's "personality." This can be done very quickly by taking a few simple tests. After we know who that creature is at the other end of the leash, I'll guide you through the steps of developing a customized regimen of basic training. Once you have taught him the basics, you can use the same methods to teach the dog whatever suits you. You can also correct the most seemingly incorrigible behavior problems.

Get ready to be surprised at how happily and reliably your friend obeys commands when you've taught him in a way that he can understand, and that shows you understand him.

Kathy Santo's Dog Sense

CHAPTER 1

"Typing" Your Dog

Admit it: You've met people and come to an instant judgment about who they are based on nothing but looks. But did you know most of us do that with dogs, too? Prejudice usually follows stereotypes about breeds.

While most training programs go along with this thinking, in my method breed is not considered. I have met pit bulls who expressed nothing like the "typical" attack dog temperament and "sweet" little toy dogs who would have you jumping on furniture to save yourself. All dogs evolved from a common ancestor, which does explain a few universal characteristics, such as the love of enclosed spaces (a carryover from cave-dwelling days). But domestication, as well as the introduction of different breeds, are relatively recent developments. It therefore makes perfect sense that breed should be a fairly weak indicator of individual nature. In fact, even less than with people, a dog's nature has little to do with what he looks like. With one exception: Size does matter.

In twenty years of training dogs, I have never met two that were exactly alike. As a matter of fact, I've never even met two that were *almost* alike. Each dog has its own unique personality. Conventional dog training prescribes a set way for teaching every new behavior. To teach a sit, for example, tradition has it you should push down on the rump saying (often repeating), "Sit!" But what if you have a dog who becomes submissive when any physical force is used to make him sit? Or, what if your dog aggressively rebels against your touching his rear end? What if you have a dog who wouldn't sit if you sat on him? These are scenarios that could quickly bring you to a dead end in conventional training. They can also generate just the sort of questions that can help you unlock your dog's personality and achieve success with my method. Now, before we proceed, a caveat: As with people, there are dogs that are simply pathological. If you have a dog whose timidity or aggression is extreme (he's not just a little put out from a thump on the rump), you should immediately seek the experience of a reputable trainer or behaviorist. If, however, you have a regular dog with regular problems who just needs to learn some manners (or unlearn some, as the case may be), then you've come to the right place. I'll ask the questions, you provide the answers, and together we'll find out what type of dog you really have: Just who is living in that furry little head?

WHY SHOULD YOU CARE WHO YOUR DOG IS?
(And no, you can't skip this section)

Mind if I ask you some personal questions? Do you care whether people know who you are? Is it important that the people in your life understand what you enjoy? Who hasn't received a present from someone dear, and groaned, "This is *so* not me!"? Even the least-self-centered person suffers when misunderstood.

Does your work environment affect your productivity? Maybe you've worked somewhere that is laid-back and mellow, when what you really needed to flourish was a high-energy, fast-paced setting. Understanding your personality type, preferences, and stimuli is vital to promoting both your contentment and your efficiency. The same goes for your dog.

What makes a dog tick varies unpredictably from individual to individual. Ignoring this fact is a surefire recipe for exasperation in training. Imagine that your dog is mainly toy motivated and you've been trying to train him by using pieces of steak as rewards. Steak is great—dogs love steak, don't they? Sure, except when they don't. What matters is this: Does your dog love the reward enough to "roll over" for it? Using the steak reward without success, you may come to a totally faulty conclusion, for instance: "That dog is so lazy, he won't even sit when I offer him STEAK!" I would guess there are thousands of dogs that have "flunked" obedience school on account of being misunderstood by their owners or trainers: for example, the emotionally sensitive dog whose owner insists on giving loud and angry-sounding commands or the low–work ethic dog whose thirty-minute training sessions would have been more effective had they been broken into three ten-minute sessions throughout the day. Such owners are convinced they are making an offer no dog could refuse. But the results speak for themselves. Assuming you can accept the basic premise that most training problems don't arise from a mental or moral deficiency, you can see where the answer to the canine-learning riddle lies. Discovering your dog's prime motivation is one of several easy diagnostic steps on the path to a successful training experience.

I use five determinants to figure out a dog's personality type.

1. **Prime Motivation:** Highly individual and unpredictable, but vital to keeping him interested in learning. I find nearly all dogs fall into one of four groups:
   - Food Motivated: Pretty self-explanatory and the one every human thinks of first.
   - Toy Motivated: "I'll do anything you want for a rubber bone."
   - Physical-Play Motivated: "Frolicking with you, running in circles, getting petted, etc.—that's my idea of living." Doesn't need a toy, just you.

- None: Responds to no stimulus yet. I say "yet" because I believe all healthy dogs have at least a latent motivation. Sometimes it's up to you to bring it out. In the sections that follow I'll give you ideas not only on how to boost the drives your dog does exhibit, but also how to uncover ones when none appear to exist. Trust me, it's in there!

2. **Energy Level:** The gauge for how long to make your training sessions. A subjective call to some degree, but I offer guidance to help you judge the level accurately.

3. **Work Ethic:** Some are decadent. Some are Calvinists. The greater the work ethic, the less the need for cheering him on and rewarding him. A dog with a naturally low work ethic will need much more of a "carrot," especially in the early stages.

4. **Emotional Sensitivity:** If you don't acknowledge it, you'll never get anywhere: Dogs have feelings, too. The highly sensitive dog needs to feel successful and, in case of an error, requires reassurance almost to the point of praise for effort alone. He must also be brought along more slowly, especially when it comes time to start testing his skills with distractions. Dogs, as well as people, who are less high-strung can naturally handle a lot more in the way of training stress.

5. **Physical Sensitivity:** When you attempt any correction, this will register right away. Some dogs respond to the slightest tug; others engage in tug-of-war. Fortunately, most dogs fall somewhere in the middle.

There is no set formula for typing your dog. And traits don't always link in ways you might expect. For example, not all emotionally sensitive dogs are physically sensitive, too. One of my favorite trainees was very tenderhearted but had the physical sensitivity of a bull elephant. He was a wheaten terrier, and terriers are known to be tenacious, but the latter fact could hardly explain this dog's blend of fragile emotions and game physicality. When the kids in his household were running around hooting and hollering, as adolescent boys will do, Beau would run off and cower in his crate. Emotionally, he was a softie. And yet, when said softie would run full tilt into the sliding glass door, fall out of the kids' tree fort (don't ask), or jump out of a parked car's open window (that was the last straw—next stop: my class), he wouldn't even blink. Moral of the story: Emotionally sensitive dogs can be physically tough. And vice versa.

PRIME MOTIVATIONS: EATING AND PLAYING, AND PHYSICAL CONTACT

Let's start with what turns *your* dog on. Try the following experiments, and record your findings.

Feed Me, Seymour!
(With apologies to the cast and crew of
Little Shop of Horrors)

Before feeding my dog dinner, I offer him a dog biscuit. He

a. looks at me as if to say, "You're kidding! James, fetch me my squeaky toy!";
b. always eats it politely;
c. scarfs it along with my pinkie;
d. goes back to sleep on the couch.

Repeat the experiment using a piece of hot dog or cheese (string cheese works best).

Feed dinner as usual.

Now, repeat the two experiments after dinner, again recording the results.

If you got all *a*'s and *d*'s, your dog is probably not very food motivated.

If you had an *a* or *d* with the biscuit but then a *b* or *c* when you switched to the hot dog or cheese, your dog is food motivated but only when given the "right" food.

If you got straight *b*'s and *c*'s, then your dog is obviously food motivated. He may also exhibit behavioral problems that include wolfing down or even audaciously stealing any food in sight, whether his or your own.

One Dog's Toy Is Another Dog's . . .

Is your dog a player? Does he make a game of fetch or tug, or does he prefer to sleep? Let's see if your dog requires a toy to have a good time. Try the following, and note your dog's reactions.

I throw a ball over my dog's head after he hasn't seen me for an hour or more. He

a. waits for me to fetch it;
b. runs and gets it but never comes back;
c. falls asleep;
d. walks away as if he thinks I'm insane;
e. fetches one to five times before losing interest;
f. fetches five to fifteen times before losing interest;
g. fetches no matter how many times I throw it (as a matter of fact it's dark, and he's still out there).

Now repeat the exercise using a tug toy or some other plaything, and record the results.

B's, *e*'s, *f*'s, and *g*'s all have a play drive, either for retrieving or tugging.

B's have a play drive; they just don't need you (after you've thrown the ball!) to have a good time. Toy-motivated dogs will play with a toy by themselves. They throw it, they chew it, they pounce on it. A playmate is optional.

We can definitely fix that.

E's have a low to average play drive.

F's have an average to high play drive; and *g*'s are compulsive players. I own one of the latter. It's wonderful because you can train them almost any time of the day or night; they are always ready for action. The downside is that they can be annoying because they constantly want—need, actually!—to be doing something. But have no fear: You can learn to harness that unusual drive in training and to redirect whatever's left toward interactive toys.

A Little to the Left

Some dogs' idea of a reward is physical contact. They don't require toys, elaborate games, or even treats. If you have one of these, you don't even need a quiz. Your dog is leaning against you at this very moment. Maybe you're even holding the book with one hand while giving your dog a tummy rub with the other. In this case, *you* are the dog's primary reward. And hey, that's good news, because unlike food- and toy-driven dogs, you'll always have your dog's motivation handy.

Dogs who are into the touchy-feely thing can be grouped into two main categories:

You Say Tomato . . .

First there are the snuggle-bunnies. They like scratches behind the ears, tummy rubs, and scritches at the base of their tails. Add verbal praise and you have doggie nirvana. This type of dog usually makes not-so-subtle suggestions that you should pet him. *Now.* And don't stop. *Ever.* Those suggestions range from leaning against you and sighing to flipping your hand up with his nose to the ever-popular hit-your-leg-with-his-paw technique. Except for flipping your hand with his nose when you are holding your morning bowl-sized cup of joe, these techniques are cute and hard to resist.

The potential downside to this type of dog is that he may be clingy; the type of dog who tries to follow you into the bathroom, and then greets you twelve seconds later like a long-lost friend. When you teach the Wait command you may find he doesn't love the idea of you being away from him. Don't worry—you'll teach him that if he can contain himself for mere minutes you'll return lavishing scratches.

I Say Tom-AH-to . . .

Then there are the roughhousers. Their tastes tend more toward the Greco-Roman wrestling style of physical contact: wrestling, pushing, and pouncing, the sort of things adolescent boys do in the middle of your living room inches from the cabinet containing your prized Capodimonte figurine collection.

While you may occasionally enjoy furnishing this type of reward, the inherent dangers are many. For those reasons, there needs to be an "on" switch, and, it goes without saying, an "off" switch.

My Border collie Quick is a roughhousing type of dog, and I have the bruises to prove it. When he was a puppy I would allow him (on a leash) to play rough with me, but when I wanted him to stop I would say "enough." If he stopped, he would get a treat. If he continued, he would get a tug on the collar. The command is now so powerful that if he's playing with my children and I notice he's getting too wild I can say "enough" from the next room and he'll chill. When he does a great job in training, I can reward him by taking him for a walk on the wild side, while still sparing myself a tiger-sized hematoma. "On" switches are nice, "off" switches are vital.

If your dog falls into the majority of canines, you have by now identified some stimuli that turn him on (and maybe off!). If he has more than one motivator, lucky you! You get to pick which one to use in training. Or you can use one type to teach one command and a second to teach the next. My personal preference is to train with food, because I can always hide a piece of food in my hand. A tennis ball or squeaky toy is a little tougher to disguise, unless you're Paul Bunyan.

If your dog shows no motivation with food, toys, or play, we'll need to dig a little deeper.

REVEALING AND BOOSTING YOUR DOG'S PRIME MOTIVATIONS
(Or, a chocolatier doesn't care to be paid in nonpareils)

If your toy- or play-drive diagnostics revealed a dog who has a "talk to the paw" attitude, there may be a very simple reason

why your dog sometimes shows no desire to play with you:
You are already his 24/7 plaything!

I had a student who *swore* her dog would never play with
her. She invited me to her house to figure out what was
"wrong" with her dog. When I arrived, I could barely get
through the door: There were eight thousand dog toys on the
floor. Stuffed animals, squeaky toys, Nylabones, Buster Cubes,
Frisbees—even a Fisher-Price toy farm (apparently the dog
liked it when Mommie opened the barn door and it went
"moo"). Pookiebear could turn any which way and grab a toy
without even coming to her feet. The use of one as a motivator
was laughable, and to make matters worse, the owner was constantly in the dog's face, asking her if she wanted to go out to
play or have some "yum-yums." The dog was overindulged
and building an increasing tolerance for being catered to—a
perfectly human, or canine, reaction.

I counseled Pookiebear's owner to pick six toys and put
away all the others in the house. Every two weeks she would
gather the six toys, drive to the U-Store-It facility, and trade
them for six new ones for the *next* two weeks. In addition, I
forbade her to praise the dog for breathing or to engage the
dog in any way unless the dog engaged her first. A very difficult (for the owner) forty-eight hours ensued as Pookiebear
moped around the house, but, miraculously, while said owner
was in the shower, Pookiebear sashayed into the bathroom and
offered up a royal bark as if to say, "Hey, why the *&^%
haven't you been playing with me?!" She had even brought a
toy with her!

The moral of this only slightly embellished story is as
follows: To spark motivation in some dogs, you have to take
some things away completely or at least cut back on them.
Sometimes that means food, sometimes that means toys, and
sometimes that means you! Yes, you. Ignoring your dog will not
kill either of you—I promise! After training is complete, you
can return to your previous habits, or you may not want to.

Here are some ideas for those of you who have dogs with
little or no food drive:

- Feed only half of the meal your dog would usually get before training. Better yet, feed him *after* training.
- Introduce more interesting food—nickel-sized slices of hot dog or string cheese can be very motivating to a dog who is restricted from having human food. Have no fear that you'll cause him to beg constantly for it (chances are he does that already). Begging happens only when the food is given directly from the table. In training, food should come from your pocket so that the dog won't become a pest every time you sit down to dinner.
- Cut back on his daily "just for breathing" treats. Use treats as rewards, not to buy love. And remember, if you worked in a chocolate factory with free-sampling privileges, you wouldn't snap to attention for chocolate either (chocoholics excepted).

CAUTION: Chocolate is a treat for humans but must never be given to dogs. It can be deadly if ingested by a canine.

Follow the same pattern with toys and play rewards: Save them for after a training session; bump them up a notch by trying something new and exciting. Most of all, get stingy. You'll not only sharpen your dog's motivations but also be able to put them to work for the both of you.

ENERGY LEVELS

When you have trained dogs for as long as I have, you develop quite a mental catalog of the characters you've met. I have seen mature dogs with the energy level of a young adult. Then there are the low-energy dogs. Some of these dogs' owners have needed nutritional counseling from their vets, and, when the dogs' diets improved, so did their energy levels. Some, after routine blood work, were discovered to have low thyroid levels and, with treatment, immediately perked up, just as humans would with the same diagnosis, and occasionally other illnesses were discovered. Some dogs were simply not active enough and needed more exercise to build up endurance. More than a few were just overweight and needed some spa therapy, a little calorie control if not a week at "Muffy Cupcake's Camp for Dumpy Dogs." Once you've established that your dog has a normal, healthy energy level, you can gear his training interval accordingly.

There are those of us who like to *play* sports, those who like to *attend* sporting events, those who like to sit on the couch *watching* sports on TV, and those who just like to sit on the couch (hold the sports). For low-energy dogs I strongly recommend short training sessions preceded by some "away time": dog alone. I am a huge proponent of the crate, which I consider the ideal "holding area" for the dog before training sessions, and will have more to say later in the book about its use. If your dog is not crate trained for pretraining separation, choose a confined area such as a small, quiet, gated-off room or an exercise pen. Such confinement ensures that your dog's energy reserve, however slight, isn't wasted jumping on furniture or investigating an interesting smell. But be careful not to use too much of a good thing. The ideal before-training crate time would be fifteen to twenty minutes; though with a subject especially apathetic toward training, the time may be increased up to an hour.

WHAT'S YOUR DOG'S WORK ETHIC?

("But I did a sit for you yesterday!")

As with a lack of food motivation, a low work ethic can be adjusted by moving the baseline. To inspire a low–work ethic dog to get with the program, you may need to cut back on or eliminate some of the contact you have with him in a normal day during the initial stages of training. Deep down, even the most blasé bichon frise considers you his ultimate stimulus— make use of that power. Keep a record of how many times you engage the dog in activities—i.e., play, petting him, talking to him—and note how many times he responds to your attentions. Cutting back almost always leads to a dog who is more appreciative of your love and ready to work to please you.

Once while teaching a beginners' class in Florida, I had a beautiful Alaskan malamute student named Serena. And serene she was, almost to the point of being terminally aloof! She gave the impression of believing she graced you with her mere presence. When you praised her, the dog would look through you with a blank stare. The offer of a treat practically elicited a yawn, and attempts at petting prompted her to walk away. Honestly, I could have done a rain dance around this dog, and she would have curled into a ball and fallen asleep. The family reported that she'd been this way since she was eight weeks old. And, no, she was not deaf or blind—she was certified as being in perfect health.

Complicating matters, Serena was a chronic runaway dog—this was the reason her family had brought her to me in the first place. Several times she had come close to being hit by a car on one of her adventures off their property. She wouldn't come, lie down, or stay for beans (or cookies or liver treats). Drastic problems call for drastic measures. I prescribed a solid week during which the family was not to speak to Serena at all except to put her leash on for walks and to put her in her crate. After the first twelve hours, the owner called to report Serena was serenely oblivious to the silent treatment. She just went about the house in her usual fashion, ignoring them all. I told her I expected as much and to keep up the good nonwork. Days two and three and four and five passed in much the same way—along with a daily phone call to report the nonprogress. At this time, Serena's family realized that she had *never* approached them to play or to be petted for the *entire* year she'd been with the family—interaction was all initiated by them and, apparently, tolerated by her.

On the sixth day I received a phone call to report Mount Serena had ERUPTED! She was throwing toys at them, nudging her nose under their hands to elicit petting, offering sit after sit after sit for the slightest word of praise or the merest treat. From that day on, everything in Serena and her family's relationship had changed. The former Greta Garbo malamute was now permanently preening for attention. And while she ultimately proved not the easiest dog to train, she was at least very easy to motivate, and more loveable once she dropped her studied indifference.

YOUR DOG'S EMOTIONAL MAKEUP?
(Jekyll and Hyde, Bonnie and Clyde)

How does he handle new situations out of the house, and how does he handle new situations in the house? The answers to these questions are important clues to the emotional makeup of your dog. At the risk of oversimplifying things, I will give you some examples of emotional types. Do you recognize your dog among them? Some temperaments are a combination of these.

Oblivious/Well-Adjusted Dog

You take the dog out for a walk, and when you return home you notice that all of your furniture has been stolen. You run for the phone, but they took that, too, and the dog calmly goes to where his bed used to be, yawns, and turns around before settling down to a nap on the bare floor. The police come, and amid their strange voices and the crackle of walkie-talkies, the dog never stirs. The kids get home from school, and he greets them in his usual manner before walking to the counter to bark until someone gives him his two o'clock dog biscuit. Thanks to the the dog gods, his biscuits haven't been stolen!

I have met many dogs like this. "Well-adjusted" would be the euphemism, and not altogether inaccurate, since the nonchalance is no danger. But what they are, for good or ill, is oblivious.

Moderate

This temperament is noted for its lack of extreme tendencies. The dog who has a moderate emotional profile would definitely notice the house has been raided and would show some signs of curiosity or mild distress at the recent turn of events. He would possibly greet the police officers with a somewhat more elaborate version of the usual greeting reserved for strangers. In short, he would react much the way you would expect a dog to react to a situation that may seem like a crisis to you but isn't a cataclysm. He registers the problem, but does not get melodramatic about it.

Sensitive/Soft

On entering an invaded house the dog of a sensitive/soft temperament would immediately sense something was terribly wrong. If this dog also possesses a high energy level, expect him to be racing around the room as if to say, "Oh my God oh my God oh my God." If you had a low-energy sensitive/soft dog, the poor thing would probably slink around the house with its tail drawn in, looking for somewhere to hide. The body language would speak of stress bottled in as opposed to channeled out. Assuming you weren't entirely cleaned out, the sensitive/soft dog might well notice before you did that something in the house was amiss.

Drama Queen/King

The drama-king dog reacts hysterically when his food and water bowls are moved five feet across the room. Thinking of a human equivalent, I always envision Linus sitting by the dryer, practically fainting as his blanket spins. The hysterical dog feels things more strongly than 99 percent of other dogs in the world. Just because *we* think it is a trivial matter to move those bowls so that we can mop under them, does that mean his feelings are not legitimate? You would never assert such a claim about a human hysteric, would you? No, feelings always have a reality of their own. However, you will have to treat the dramatic type of dog in an upbeat and reassuring manner. Banish the ever-so-tempting "Oh, my sweetums, what has Mommie done to you wittle bowlsie-wowlsies?" This is not helpful and can actually validate the dog's anxiety, to say nothing of driving up a wall everyone who must listen to this prattle!

Emotional makeup is key to structuring the entire training process. Sensitive dogs generally do better with more frequent but shorter sessions. They may need a little more paw holding, occasionally a break (even during a short training session). They also need to be trained in the greatest variety of locations if they are to grow accustomed to obeying in unfamiliar environments. Start slow (an empty playground) and work up to busier environments (a bustling park, a party). Consistency and constant encouragement will help the sensitive dog progress from worried to confident.

When you enter the distraction phase of training you'll start to teach your dog in what situations you expect him to obey. The answer, he'll discover, is that he should obey you in ALL situations. During this time, the sensitive dog will need a lot more cheerleading than the average dog and, in some extreme cases, a little praise just for trying—an A for effort.

A WORD ABOUT VERBAL PRAISE . . . QUIET!!!!!!!!!!!!!!!!!!!!!!!!!!!!!!

Among the few perfect common denominators: Dogs do have better hearing than we do. So try to avoid out-Heroding Herod. While there are dogs who appreciate loud, boisterous praise, most are happier with a soft "atta boy" or "goood dog." Generally, confident and oblivious dogs don't believe the hype, while a shy, sensitive type will get frightened and may even shut down. Either way, you're well served with a sotto voce approach.

GNASHING OF TEETH! BEATING OF BREASTS!
(And some dog training, too)

Just as dogs differ in emotional sensitivity, their physical sensitivity varies a good deal, too. Like many humans (especially some males!), some dogs have no tolerance for pain. On the soft end of the scale we have those dogs who, if they trip on rocks, will fall whimpering, even wailing, to the ground. But on the other end there are those who can use their heads inadvertently to block the game-winning goal at a professional soccer game and keep trotting along as if nothing has happened. Most dogs fall somewhere in the middle. Do note that physical sensitivity is not breed or size related. There are just as many fragile Great Danes as there are scrappy toy poodles.

When the time comes to apply a physical correction, it needs to be measured based on a sense of your own dog's sensitivity to it. He has to have understood what he was asked to do (otherwise it seems a gratuitous infliction of discomfort), and it has to be clear to him that he failed to obey, regardless of whether he was distracted or just didn't feel like obeying. (Your clue that the dog has a clear understanding of a command will be a very high rate of correct responses in your early, noncorrective training stages.) The perfect correction (degree of force) will depend on how physically sensitive (or insensitive) your dog has shown himself to be. Too rough and the more sensitive dog will shut down; too gentle and the tough dog will brush it off ("Was that a mosquito?").

Trying to educate my clients that dogs *need* to be corrected (that there are consequences for not obeying) can be quite challenging. (I suspect the same people may have problems in child rearing, but that's another field.) I have a student who cannot, nay, WILL NOT correct SnookyBaBa no matter how many times I point out that SnookyBaBa will soon be pushing up doggy daisies if he doesn't quit running into traffic. Then there are also the equally self-defeating "car-alarm" dog owners. Their philosophy before training with me was to scream "No!" earsplittingly until the dog "listened." Ironically, SnookyBaBa is usually a dog oblivious to any correction more subtle than a firehose, and for all their indifference to incessant noise, many dogs owned by the car alarmers would faint if you looked at them harshly. Nature definitely has a sense of humor.

. . .

How can you judge your dog's specific physical sensitivity? There is a test commonly done on puppies (and aptly called the physical-sensitivity test). The tester holds the puppy and gently squeezes the webbing between the dog's toes, noting how much of a squeeze it takes to make the puppy register discomfort. The phrase "register discomfort" is important here—dogs don't always yelp or scream or writhe. Please note: We don't want them at the point of yelping, screaming, or writhing in training! This is America! Sometimes during the test, the dog will chew at the tester's hand, which may not be an indication of discomfort but merely a response to the foot being held. This test can be hard to perform yourself, so you may want to leave it to a professional if you remain uncertain about your dog's sensitivity level (it's crucial to get this right). Alternatively, you could assume your dog has an average physical sensitivity and, when you are in the correcting stage of training, begin all your corrections mildly. You can always escalate, if needed. A correction is something a dog should work to avoid. An ineffective correction is one that scares the dog, hurts the dog, or simply goes unnoticed.

I *LOVE* THIS JOB!
(Except when I don't!)

Most dogs, not just those in the so-called working group, love to work. As a matter of fact, the canine desire to please is what makes people want to have dogs as pets. Difficulty in training a dog rarely comes from his lacking this basic characteristic and usually comes from a problem in his understanding and executing what is expected of him. My method teaches dogs how to think, how to learn, allowing them to maintain for all their lives that innately happy attitude toward doing as they are told. When your dog learns that he will be praised, fed, and/or played with when he obeys your commands, the work becomes even *more* rewarding to him.

But there is no way to get there without correction. Period. Corrections do take many forms. For one dog it might be withholding a reward, be it praise or a dog cookie, while another will never get the message without a "pop" on the leash. The universal rule however is this: Correction must NEVER be enacted in anger (dogs can tell, and it's counterproductive), and proper correction is *never* abusive!

Correction isn't intended to alter a dog's psyche or scar him for life; such eventuality can only dissolve the bond between animal and owner. Correction is an instructive tool, administered after the dog has thoroughly learned a behavior (to sit, to come when called, etc.). And in the case of behavior problems posing an immediate health threat (car chasing, for instance), it's a stopgap until more comprehensive training can be undertaken (dog triage demands you stop the bleeders before tending the ones with splinters).

People have told me that they could no more correct their dog with a pop on the leash than discipline their children with a slap on the hand. To compare corporal punishment of children with physical correction in training dogs is simply ludicrous. Dogs have a different code of conduct; for example, a mother dog will "scruff shake" her puppy to discipline it. That's a physical correction, not a discussion! It's totally unemotional, with no anger attached to it at all—just a standard form of canine communication. Humans, on the other hand, have been given a wonderful gift called speech with which to educate their young, so even the benign physical correction is unnecessary in my child-rearing experience. While dogs do need physical correction, the degree is all-important. I must declare myself as coming from the "no hitting" school of thought for dogs as well as children. If you'll forgive a mother's pride, I can report that my children are very happy, well-mannered, loving, and decent little human beings. And without undue professional pride, I am pleased to report that my dogs are very happy, well-mannered, loving, and decent little canines. The training methods for each group may have been very different, but the overall results are the same (although my dogs still can't carry their bowls to the sink after dinner!).

However, physical correction is only one element of my method. And, as with every other part of the training, it works only when you've bothered to discover who your dog is. Only then can your dog learn effectively and happily.

YOU CALL THIS A REWARD?

Please name for me the five things a dog would most likely perceive as a reward. Okay, name just the top three. I know, I know: "Hey, I didn't buy this book to be asked a lot of tricky questions." Please bear with me, and name three.

Okay. Let's check your answers. Did you perhaps include at least one of the following: food, pats/scratches, toys, and words of praise? Indeed, all the above are widely recognized among dogs as being rewards. But that doesn't mean each of these will float every dog's boat. Most employees love to get a raise. But some think that they work too hard and you simply couldn't pay them enough to work any more. They value something else more than they value the most obvious reward typically thrown at them. So it is sometimes with dogs as well. To a dog who isn't a "workhorse" a reward might be *not* having to do another sit. It might even be Aunt Bessie's shriek as she tumbles to the floor when Pookiebear jumps on her at full steam. (Sometimes rewards are not in the eye of the rewarder. Sometimes, too, bad behavior is its own reward, so that even a correction for, say, a hit-and-run on Aunt Bessie is ineffective because the deed was so sweet, not to mention already savored, that it was worth whatever grief you'll give Pookiebear for it.)

Of Rewards and Corrections: The Calculus of Acting Up

Like all of us, dogs are frequently engaged in cost-benefit analysis. As you may know, a number of manufacturers produce a so-called hidden fence. A wire is buried in the ground (hence "hidden") and connected to a power source. The dog wears a special collar and is taught that when he gets too close to the fence line the collar will beep. If he continues moving into the "red zone," he will receive a mild to moderate electric shock. For many dogs this is an effective deterrent. Of course, your dog may not care about a little pain as long as he can chase the car or squirrel or cat or jogger. Such a dog may willingly take the "hit" of the fence, knowing that, if he can run far enough, the correction will stop and he will be *free*—at least until you pantingly catch up to him. The fence zap that some dogs would receive as a major correction seems to others like merely a speed bump. Because response to correction varies from canine to canine, effective training depends absolutely on discovering your particular dog's comfort zone—this is defined by both his pleasures (the things for whose enjoyment he'll do whatever you want) and his personal deterrents (the things, other than physical abuse, that he *in particular* finds so distasteful as to make him refrain from the bad behavior he may love just to avoid what always follows). Frequently, neither type of stimulus is as obvious as you might expect. So suspend your received wisdom about rewards (treats, scratches, and atta-boys) and corrections (yelling NO or relegating him to the fenced yard) if the customary gestures seem less than effective.

My Border collie Trigger's favorite reward is a game I call Run, Run, Run (original, no?). When she does whatever I've asked, as a reward I allow her to run frantically in a circle around me. Did I train Trigger to run around me? Nope. But when I observed her doing it of her own free will, I opportunistically attached a command to the behavior. Now, in training, she's permitted to do it only on command. Observe your dog, and find her natural bliss. Then turn that into a reward.

Some dogs love high-pitched squealing praise or a good game of tug. Wrestling on the ground is also very popular. Toy access cannot be underestimated if your dog is really attached to whatever old shoe or rubber duck you may have. The key is to observe your dog when he is just being himself. When he doesn't realize you're watching him, that's the time to figure out his ruling passions.

Couldn't you really use a coffee break about now? Okay, so dogs don't drink coffee, but a break during the training session can be a real treat if your dog is somewhat ambivalent about training, if it's not yet his favorite pastime. How would he react if, after a perfect sit, you praised him, brought him back into the house (or your fenced yard), took off his leash and collar, and said, "You're done!"? The ultimate three-minute training session—a sit and that's it. Now, if you expect to have your dog trained before he's ten years old, making this the rule isn't very efficient. Nevertheless, the occasional break from a more rigorous training pattern can produce gratifications for him that carry over into the next training session. By contrast, of course, a dog who loves training and thrills to the food/toy reward would NOT feel rewarded by breaking a session after one sit. Knowing *your* dog is the key to getting the most out of your training sessions. Is there a potential drawback to leisure as reward? A bit of one possibly. Don't be surprised if just as you begin your next session he seems to be saying, "Okay, I did a sit, so I'm done." But the rewards will eventually outweigh any initial confusion. You don't expect a jackpot every time you pull a slot-machine handle. But if you've had the rush of winning once, you will more than likely play again. So it is with dogs. How many rewards of whatever kind will be necessary to fuel interest and keep him working harder and harder?—that all depends on who your dog is!

HI-IQ K9?

Almost everyone seems to wish, pray for, and imagine himself to have a highly intelligent dog, the pinnacle of canine achievement, right? (As with children, the alternative scenario is too much for some adults even to contemplate.) Well, I have a news flash for all those people—a dog is not a child! There's no canine Ivy League. They don't even make bumper stickers that say "My Dog Is on the Honor Roll." In fact, while intelligence and success in life do correlate for children, practically speaking, a high-IQ dog can be relatively difficult to train. He might catch on to a concept quickly, but he can also get bored twice as fast. And, if you are not absolutely precise and consistent in training, the Hi-IQ K9's powers to perceive slight differences may only cause him to muddle the training, creating more problems than you expected. ("Hmmm, wasn't he standing on my left last time? Wonder what 'sit' means when he's on my right?" Argh!)

Misunderstandings can enter the basic programming very easily—you must be on the lookout. One of my students came to class and announced that she had taught her clever mastiff to sit in five minutes! That sounds like quite a feat, except that every time the dog sat, he would take his big ol' mastiff paw and swipe the owner on the leg. His owner was a bit sheepish when this defect in the dog's obedience was pointed out; she was simply so proud that her obviously brilliant canine had mastered a skill that she was prepared to ignore the rough edge. I observed this behavior a few more times. Sure enough, every time the dog sat and whomped his owner's leg, he got a treat. The owner believed she was rewarding the sit, but the dog had calculated that the reward depended on delivering the sit *plus* a good thump. So the owner was not merely ignoring the misdeed, she was actually *rewarding* it. It took only twenty minutes to uncouple the thump-reward connection, and in that time I stressed two basic ideas:

1. It doesn't matter what *we* think we are rewarding the dog for, but rather what the *dog* thinks we are rewarding him for. (Reread that twice, then twice more for posterity.)
2. (A corollary to concept 1) Sometimes the answer to a training problem is simply a matter of learning to see the situation as the dog sees it.

In the end, dog training is more like first grade than Mensa. A dog genius is not much good if he won't apply himself. High IQ is an overrated (and overasserted) canine virtue. If you want to use one of those fabled three wishes, ask for a strong work ethic!

BIG GUY, LITTLE GUY

Size is the easiest characteristic to diagnose. You've heard of big dogs who act like little dogs, and little dogs who act like big dogs, but I'm not referring to psychology, just simple geometry. In some cases when you're training, you will need to make adjustments to angle of approach, degree of force, etc., all depending on your dog's physical stature. Keep an eye out for those situations in which you will have to calibrate according to his needs.

"SONS OF *&%$#—BUMPUSES!!!!"
(Or, "A word to the wise")

If the above reference is unfamiliar, you've probably never left the TV on all day on December 25. *A Christmas Story* (1983) is a broadcast perennial during the winter holiday season. It's a good rental, too. I love it for many reasons, but as a dog trainer I'm a sucker for the relationship between the father and his neighbors' dogs, the Bumpus hounds. Near the end of the movie, the Bumpus pack—about a dozen smelly, barky, ill-behaved bloodhounds who make the father's life a living hell—crash through the back door and steal the much-anticipated, just-out-of-the-oven Christmas turkey. This is when the father, virtually apoplectic at the loss of his beloved bird, utters his immortal words as the dogs, having picked the carcass clean, rampage back out the door

"Sons of *&%$#—Bumpuses!!!!"

Most dog owners have been "Bumpus-hound mad" at one

point or another. Dogs sometimes behave in ways unacceptable to humans. But how you react should be guided by common sense. By a certain age, a child can be reasoned with as to *why* he shouldn't take a fat marker to Mommie's new tricolored, faux-finished, four-thousand-dollar living-room wall, and can be told *what* will happen to him the next time he expresses his creativity that way. In general, a child will eventually see things as you do, and you will feel better about everything (except perhaps the repainting bill!). But I promise you with every fiber of my being that you will never get anywhere by sitting down to reason with your dog about the heartbreak caused by his peeing on your oriental rug. People do tell me, "Oh, but the dog looks so regretful when I scold him." Rest assured, he is reacting to nothing but the tone of your voice. If you don't believe me, try telling him something witheringly negative in the sweet, chirpy voice you use for praise. "When I came home from work, opened the front door, and slid through that pile of poop you left in the hallway, I wanted to kill you, you wretched cur!" Watch your dog wag his tail and cock his head without the least sign of stress. By the same token, if you screamed at him in your most menacing voice, saying, "What a good dog! You are the best! I love you," your dog would probably cower in fear. (If you want a well-trained dog, take my word for it and don't test this phenomenon at home.) A word to the wise should be sufficient: Dogs mainly respond to tone. And when your tone is one of tension and distress, it can take over the poor dog's brain, preventing him from processing or taking direction. For this reason, you must always strive to react without emotion whenever correcting your dog.

Setup: You're about to sit down to a fat sirloin when you realize that you don't have a steak knife. Sighing heavily, you stand and take three steps to the knife drawer; no sooner have you plucked the necessary implement than you turn around to discover your dog has sat down to your dinner. . . . I know what you *want* to do (considering you are now armed and dangerous), but take a deep breath and count to three (four, if it's filet mignon). Now, reach over, grab his collar, and remove his face from your plate. But don't do it with anger! (Try very hard.) You must pull him in such a way as to force him to conclude, "I don't like that, and I won't be dining here again!" but not "Oh, my God, what have I done? The world is coming to an end!" A correction should be something a dog wants to avoid, but not so traumatic he can't remember the cause of it. The latter is not only ineffective but undermines your whole relationship with him.

Now—brace yourself—having separated his face from your plate, you have to *praise* him for getting off the table! Desirable behavior must be immediately reinforced just as undesirable behavior must be instantly censured. If you don't make clear to the dog what you'd rather he be doing, he will invent his own alternatives, which, chances are, won't be any more acceptable than the original foul deed.

The next step in training involves testing to see whether the correction has taken. Yes, try it with your backup sirloin immediately. There is always a chance that it hasn't, and you may have to escalate the correction, with a sharper tug. Meanwhile, don't take your eyes off the steak.

You are not doing your dog, much less yourself (as a dog *and* steak lover), any favors when you delay in pointing out unacceptable behavior. Have you ever seen a wildlife video on wild-dog or wolf packs? Watch what happens when one of them gets out of line. I'll tell you this much: They don't sit on a rock and berate one another, and they *certainly* don't discuss who "owns" the problem. The wayward pack member is corrected in a decisive physical manner, and it's done. No sulking, no grudges. Point taken. Some people could take a page from the wolves' book on releasing anger after a disagreeable situation is over. Dog emotions are entirely of the moment, while human emotions are all too often in the past (bitter memories) or future (dreaded prospects). Through practice I have learned to make a correction on a dog without feeling or expressing anger before, during, or after the incident. In fact, I have come to appreciate that even if there is a perfect reason for strong emotion (as in, "He ate my steak; now I'm eating Cheerios") the dog is the last "person" I would ever want to know it. Don't confuse him; in his mind, the event is over. So don't be surprised if he ignores your pique (even more maddening). Dogs are without guilt or bourgeois scruples. It will *never* impress your dog to hold up the evidence of his crime with verbal reproaches such as "What were you thinking? These were brand-new! They cost a fortune!"

Correct without anger and praise immediately when he's got it right. It's that simple.

STACKING THE BISCUITS IN YOUR FAVOR

While I'm preaching "grin and bear it," let me also offer some empowerment points. Your training session will be hugely more effective if you remember them.

1. Generally, the ideal mental state (I mean the dog's) for the purposes of training is hungry, lonely, and/or bored. Awake helps, too! The dog that has just had a large meal, has been interacting with the family, or has enjoyed an hour of playtime will not typically be interested in working. For dogs with higher food or play drives this maxim may not apply, or may apply to a lesser degree. The stronger your dog's drive, the less you need to deprive him to inspire motivation.
2. New exercises/behaviors are best learned in a quiet location without distractions for you or the dog. (Kids at school, answering machine on!)
3. Progress depends on clear goals. Know your goal, be sure it's realistic, and stick to it. You can't teach several skills in one session. You usually can't teach even one completely. Your chances of success are better if you decide ahead of time what you want to accomplish and stay on that path. However . . .
4. Be flexible and backtrack when needed. Sometimes

the best-laid plans fall short. Recently I was going to teach my dog Quick how to lie down, when I observed he seemed to have forgotten how to sit properly! I couldn't ignore the faulty sit, the first, most basic skill, so rather than teach the down, I spent the time fixing his sit. Don't be defeated by the need for remedial work; it's par for the course. Dog training is not a rite of passage; it's a lifelong process.

5. Quit before your partner does. Timing your session is absolutely critical! Decide how long you are going to spend, and don't go over. In fact, if your dog seems tired out, end the session sooner. Rule of thumb: Quit when the dog is still eager to continue. Leave 'em wanting more, and they'll be all the keener for the next session. In terms of real time, I recommend fifteen to twenty minutes a day for adult dogs and ten to fifteen minutes for puppies, and I recommend that you set aside thirty minutes in which to accomplish those fifteen-or-so "active" minutes. You can do two such sessions a day if you find your dog willing.

6. In the mood: Train when *you* are happy! If you are not feeling 100 percent then reschedule the session. Remember being in class with a teacher who was having a bad day? A dog can sense how you feel, and your session will go downhill fast. Why make it harder on yourself anyway?

PATIENCE, PATIENCE, AND PATIENCE
("How long can this go on?")

The forty-five-minute baked potato is a thing of the past. Fork it, pop it in the microwave, and in eight minutes or less you have what you want. I know people who can't use the phone without speed dial. Even at Disney World, where the long lines are as famous as the rides, the new view of time has arrived. With a FastPass you can pick a ride, pick a time, come back, and bypass the line. Being a big fan of Disney (and baked potatoes), I love these innovations. Unfortunately, a dog is not a potato, and training one is hardly an amusement-park ride (though, on occasion, closer than you might think). Training your dog correctly and thoroughly takes time, patience, and persistence.

Patience comes into play two ways. First, in teaching. No screaming, hitting, or tearing your hair out. Teaching a dog is more than teaching him discrete behaviors; it is also showing him *how* to learn, and that can take time—a lot of time. Think back to when you had to learn something difficult—a piano piece, for instance. You probably felt the stress of working very hard to "get it." Whether you know how to play the "Moonlight" sonata or not, my guess is that if someone shoved you and screamed "NO!" every time you made a mistake, you wouldn't have learned any more quickly. Now, imagine that your piano teacher spoke no English! You would have appreciated all the patience he or she could muster as you struggled to understand the lesson without the benefit of mutually understood words. Absent such patience, you'd have probably quit, at least in your heart, where your spirit was broken. Pity your dog, who can't quit the class, however much he might like to. You and he will progress quickly and happily if you are patient and understanding with him.

Like staying in shape, dog training is a long-term project, not an eight-week boot camp. In eight weeks you can teach some important skills, but you will have really only just scratched the surface of what the dog can (and needs to) learn. Over time you will reinforce the old as you introduce improvement and refinements. Done properly, training can be a wonderfully rewarding interaction between you and your pet, the pleasure of better mutual understanding lifting the effort far above more mundane (though important) chores, such as picking up poop. As with any nonmechanical system, there will be mistakes, and some degree of canine error is as unavoidable as human error.

My student Axle, a Yorkshire terrier, weighed about four pounds soaking wet. He was dangerously cute but would not stay for love or money. If Mommie was leaving, so was Axle. For eight weeks, his owner focused mightily on convincing Axle that it was okay for him to *stay* at the end of a twenty-six-foot flexi leash. Meticulously, she reinforced the concept that nothing bad would happen to him, and Mommie would come back. Eventually we had Axle doing a three-minute stay in a line of dogs, all outweighing him by at least fifty pounds. He understood his job and was doing his stays like a pro! Then came Graduation Day, when Axle's owner sat him in the line of dogs, just as she had been doing for the past two months. She left him to sit and stay, just as she had done about a hundred times before, and when she got to the end of her flexi, like the rest of the handlers in her class, she put the handle down on the ground. Unfortunately, *unlike* the other handlers, Mommie forgot to lock her flexi. Anyone who understands the spring action of a retractable leash can guess what happened next: The case went flying, with laser-guided precision, toward the dog. The impact was decisive: Had Mommie been bowling, not dog-training, someone would have yelled, "Strrrike!" It took Axle another eight weeks to reestablish trust in the safety of sit/stay, another four before he would let Mommie go the full distance away from him. Big-picture lesson: You will make mistakes, and your dog will be okay in spite of you. The same dog brain that forgets the most painstaking lesson will also forgivingly forget the occasional trauma. Few are scarred for life. (Little-picture lesson: Always lock your flexi before you put it on the ground! It's been about ten years, and Axle's mother still has the occasional flashback.)

IT HAPPENS IN THE BEST OF FAMILIES

Let's pretend for a minute that you've finished the book, done the training, and you now have a trained dog. The work is done and, oh, is your dog something to behold. A thing of beauty. A work of art. You are the envy of your neighbors and not a little pleased with yourself as trainer extraordinaire. You scoff at those unruly beasts (especially Mr. Murphy's hideous little dog, Twisty) you see dragging their owners around the neighborhood. Life is good. Then one Sunday morning at six a.m., you get up as usual to take Angel-Face out for his morning walk. After hooking the leash to his collar and pouring yourself a big mug of coffee you tiptoe out to the backyard to let the dog take care of business while you stand watch in your pajamas and slippers. The first thing you notice is the sensation of flying, next is the sensation of falling, followed immediately by the sensation of great pain. While you were in your morning fog, Angel-Face saw a squirrel and took off, yanking you and your morning coffee halfway across the lawn. Still flat on your back, you look up and see Angel-Face's caboose flying down the road in hot pursuit of his prey. You race after him, screaming, "Angel, come! Angel, COME! ANGEL, CO-O-O-O-ME!" It would appear Angel-Face has assumed an alias, or else has suffered a bout of amnesia; in any case, he shows no recognition of the words "Angel" or "come." You test the name-change theory, screaming, "*&%$@ it, I said come!!!" as you continue running after him. Journeying through the neighborhood, you notice your neighbors peering out their windows. Peering and pointing. And laughing. Some are on the phone, apparently spreading the word of this spectacle. You have yet even to notice the grass stain that starts from your neck and runs down the length of your left leg— this will never wash out, but you are already wondering whether the limp you've developed since the fall is permanent. After a few blocks, you will also question why you have a dog and what kind of lawyer you should hire to sue the trainer. Just then you remember: *You* are the dog's trainer. Your moment of recognition is broken as you pass by Mr. Murphy's house, out in front of which is Twisty, gyrating at the end of his leash as usual. In your direction, Neighbor Murphy yells, "Run, Forrest, run!" (It's payback time.) When you finally catch up with Angel-Face, you drag him home by the collar, pour yourself another cup of coffee, and collapse on the couch to watch in numb horror as the dog takes his morning poop in the middle of your living room.

Welcome to rock bottom. The local time is seven a.m.

Relax. We've all been there. Why do trained dogs go bad? Well, the simple answer is that stuff happens. Sometimes the dog has been doing the same routines in the same places and just gets bored. Sometimes people get lax, tolerating sloppy obedience. Or, they haven't trained thoroughly enough, and the dog really doesn't understand the whole concept. Your dog comes when you call him from your living room when the house is quiet? Well, unless you live on a deserted island, that's not good enough. If that's the only situation when he reliably obeys the command to come, don't be shocked when he goes racing after another dog and ignores your call. In this case the training has not been varied enough. Or perhaps not strict enough: I have students who are frustrated that their dogs won't come the first time they call, yet they will admit to giving the command no fewer than five times before physically enforcing it. Dogs need a credible deterrent to disobedience if they are to acknowledge that "come" means they better come and "sit" means they darn well better sit.

Another reason for training breaking down is age—more specifically, the ages from five months up to two years. Not all dogs go through this adolescence. In some it can last just a month. Others will be Rebels Without a Cause for the full two years. I always expect to see some sort of rebellion in a dog of any age. That's just spirit. The point is to manage it for both your benefits.

Most training breakdowns aren't due to spontaneous combustion. In all likelihood good form has been disintegrating little by little without your noticing, much less correcting it. An eagle eye is necessary to keeping up appearances as well as realities. Take my student's standard poodle, Raven. She learned quickly and eagerly—she was a natural. Then midway through her training, I went off to teach an obedience camp in Seattle for two weeks. I returned to discover that in the interim, Raven had developed a serious sit-stay problem. First, let me define what the dog is expected to do in this exercise: sit and wait. Really, that's it. No moving feet, no shifting hip to hip, no whirling dervish, no sniffing the ground, no whining or barking. Other than sitting, she may turn her head from side to side as long as her body doesn't budge.

Why am I so rigid about staying? First, the AKC's (American Kennel Club) competition sit-stay exercise is written that way, and if you want to obtain your AKC obedience competition titles, the dog must be in exact compliance. But even more important is the "broken-window principle": Let them get away with a little "harmless" shifting and fidgeting, and before you know it they're breaking the sit.

Now, back to Raven . . . Her owner put her on a sit-wait and walked to the other side of the yard. Before she had gotten five feet away, Raven shifted onto her hip. Her owner, oblivious because her back was turned, did nothing. When she reached the end of the yard, she turned around and smiled at Raven. The dog probably thought, "It's okay if I shift my hip—my mom is so happy about it that she's smiling!" Next, Raven, seeing something behind her, rotated ninety degrees counterclockwise. Then she scratched her ear. Still no word from her owner. Finally, Raven got up and started to walk away, at which point her owner went in to correct her for breaking the stay. It was obvious to me, when I observed Raven being allowed to do all these subversive little things, that she was far from doing a focused stay. But the owner hadn't noticed anything wrong before she saw the need to intervene. For all the feedback she was getting, Raven could have been reading a book and having a latte and still would not have known she was doing a poor job of sitting.

I explained to Raven's mom my theory and asked her to keep a close eye on the sit/wait—correcting for every movement not in the precise definition of stay and seeing what happens. By the end of the week, Raven's stay problem had disappeared. Our dogs know only what we tell them—either by our actions or inaction. Here's a good basic rule for you to remember:

If, once you have finished training,
your dog doesn't respond to your command the first time,
it's your fault,
and if he doesn't respond quickly enough,
it's your fault,
and if he outright disobeys,
it's your fault,
and if he is too distracted to listen,
it's your fault.

Basically, everything comes back to you, so accept the responsibility if you expect to be leader of the pack.

With Apologies to The Who . . .

Whooo are you?
Who? Who?
Who? Who?

Well, if you've done the work, now you know. Or at least, you certainly have a better idea of your dog's character profile. You have a sense whether his temperament is stable, sensitive, or dramatic. You know to what degree his boat is floated by food and/or toys or play or just you being you. If your dog seems not of this world and doesn't want *some*thing, your first task is to *make* him want something! Look deep into his eyes. If he is a Pookiebear (spoiled darling), take away some toys, reduce or eliminate the treats, and hang back on the face time. If your dog has a crate and is ambivalent about training, I recommend putting him in the cooler for an hour before and a half hour following each session. Great leadership means inspiring motivation. I know you can do it!

CHAPTER 2

The Five "W's" of Training

The Who, What, Where, When, Why (and How) of Training

Welcome to the beginning! If you've made it here to the training section, your commitment (or at least your desperation) is still intact. We are ready to get under way, so let's lay out the most fundamental principles of training, which are easy to remember by borrowing the old journalistic saw "Who, what, where, when, and why."

WHO TRAINS THE DOG?

I advise that initially there be only one person in charge of teaching the commands. He or she can pass on all established ground rules (such as giving only one command at a time) to other family members. It's all right for others to address the dog, but in the beginning stages, only one person should be the teacher. Once the dog has been responding reliably for about a week to that person's command—for example, "sit"—then you can bring in the rest of the family. Bear in mind, however, that if there is a "weak link" in your family—a person who gives a command and doesn't enforce it—the dog will suffer to the degree that he perceives he has the choice to obey or not. I have seen families of six in which a dog would listen to only one of them. This is not acceptable, but you have to get your family to go by the book if you expect your dog to do so. As for the oft-heard assertion that the dog will prefer people who don't train him, this is pure myth. Good training should be a positive experience, so the dog's closest bond is typically to the one who has trained him.

WHAT DO I TEACH FIRST?

Sit. No, not you, your dog. The first command the dog learns when you use my training method marks the first attempt your dog will make at learning *how* to learn. It is the foundation of all things. It is also the behavior she will resort to most often when she wants your attention or a reward. If you're having trouble with some later skill, you will welcome the accomplished sit as a "reset button," and you could do worse than to have a dog that at least greets your family and your guests by sitting rather than jumping up—generally more pleasant for all parties. Now I know some of you are saying, "My dog *knows* how to sit. I need to get him to come when I call!" Most people *think* their dog understands "sit," but in reality there are usually big holes in the compliance, just waiting to reveal themselves at the most inopportune moment. A dog who completely understands the "sit" command will do it anywhere, anytime, the first time she is told. Anything less than that and you should assume she needs to be retaught. You can't fool around with the foundation of all things.

WHERE DO I TRAIN?

Train in a quiet environment, at first. But as soon as the dog has the concept of the particular command—he responds correctly to it immediately and consistently—you should take your show on the road. I don't mean the interstate, but rather the next room, then the next, then the backyard, front yard, and side yard. In the advanced stages you will go to parks that allow dogs, soccer games, walking trails, all for the purpose of showing your dog that you expect him to obey the command no matter where he is. Obviously he can't *know* that unless you take him somewhere new to test the training. If he ignores you, whether on account of distraction or imagined choice (ha!), you correct immediately. Only by his mistakes and your corrections can he fully learn the difference between right and wrong.

WHEN DO I TRAIN?

Do a session when you have an uninterrupted half hour to devote totally to your dog's training—and only when you're dog is hungry, lonely, and/or bored. *Don't* train if you're in a lousy mood, overtired, or absolutely have to bring the kids to a soccer game in twenty minutes. Always block out thirty minutes: If you get everything done in fifteen, great! If not (more typical scenario) you won't have to abort without having taken care of business. Train at least three days a week; five days is better; seven days is optimal. Wait! Before you chuck this book in the trash, read this: When your dog is fully trained (a few months from now), you'll be in maintenance mode. Then you'll just need to do occasional "refresher" sessions to keep him in tip-top obedient shape. Since this method actually works, you won't need to devote the next ten years of your life to daily dog training. Aren't you relieved?

WHY?

See under "Sons of *&%$#—Bumpuses!!!!," page 25. Anyone can live with an untrained dog in theory, but consider your quality of life, and the poor creature's.

HOW WILL I BECOME THE VERY BEST TRAINER I CAN BE?

By making mistakes. By paying attention to your dog—that means watching his body language for signs of stress, confusion, and/or fear. This may *seem* a lot to think about, but it becomes automatic with surprisingly little practice (this is your training, too!). Good training becomes less a set of rules and more a mind-set you can enter with ease. To learn how, you need to read this book through before you even snap a leash on your dog.

Throughout, bear in mind that every dog is different, just as every person is different. When you factor in family peculiarities, socioeconomic variations, weather conditions, and lunar cycles, it becomes clear that no two dog-and-handler teams are even remotely alike! Honor the unique qualities that you and your dog both bring to the training, and you'll find the balance between a loosey-goosey relationship and a dictatorship. Don't worry; I'll be quite clear about what's not negotiable, for instance: Until your dog is "Master of Sit," he's not going anywhere and neither are you. And this above all: Love your dog!

CHAPTER 3

Equipment

A BUCKLE COLLAR

The fit of a collar should be snug but not tight. If you can slide two fingers under the collar, that's perfect. For growing puppies, remember to check the fit every week. If you must have tags on this collar, please secure them together with clear tape. I know, I know—you like the jingle because it tells you where the dog is, but your dog is not a cow, and this is for his comfort, not yours! Your dog's jingling tags are the equivalent of you wearing your house and car keys as a set of earrings. In fact it's even worse because dogs have better hearing than we do.

Other Training Collars

If you have a dog that offers extreme resistance to being walked in a buckle collar, which is unusual, there is a range of alternatives, from head halters (which are ineffective for teaching "sit," "down," etc., but can help with a dog who pulls during a walk) to prong collars, an interlocking chain of blunt metal prongs connected by a loop of small chain link. This collar, when tightened, evenly applies pressure around a dog's neck. Both of these can be effective but should only be introduced under the guidance of a professional dog trainer. He or she can precisely assess the dog's response to the respective stimuli and can help you make an informed choice as to the equipment best for your dog.

A FOUR- TO SIX-FOOT LEASH

Nylon, leather, anything but a chain leash will do—it's a dog walk, not a perp walk! I prefer a four-foot because it's easier to handle, but some people like the six-footer. Large dogs need a wide leash; small and medium-sized dogs need a much narrower one. For small dogs, make sure that the bolt (the clip that attaches to his collar) is a reasonable size. You don't want your four-pound dog's chin drooping because he effectively has a millstone hanging around his neck.

Avoid leashes without bolt clips. Parrot clips can slip off collar rings.

Retractable Leash

There are many retractables on the market—choose wisely. I find the cheap ones are not at all sturdy. My personal preference is the flexi brand. Get the twenty-six-foot length, and stay away from the ones with flashlights! You will not be doing any coal mining.

A GREAT SELECTION OF TRAINING MOTIVATORS

If you yourself are your dog's favorite toy, then—lucky you!—nothing else is necessary. Those with low-to-moderate food-driven dogs will have no success with any treats the dog gets all day long just for looking cute. You have to upgrade the treats (and while you're at it, stop rewarding cuteness and start rewarding performance): sliced hot dogs made from chicken or turkey, bits of cheese sticks, Cheerios, etc. One of my students uses tortellini with her dog. Hey, whatever works (just make sure the tortellini aren't frozen).

If you have a toy-motivated dog, use toys that the dog *never sees* except when you are training. It makes the toys— and therefore the training—extra-exciting. Small fabric Frisbees can be easily concealed. Tennis balls and (fake) squeaky mice (terriers love them) are great, but sometimes you have to de-squeak them so that the toy itself doesn't become a distraction in the learning stage.

FOR ADVANCED DOGS—A THIRTY- TO FIFTY-FOOT LIGHT LINE

This leash is made up of a really tiny bolt attached to a really light line—hence the name. You can make it yourself out of nylon or polypropylene line, but remember, it's *NOT for tugging*! Read and reread the section "Hanging by a Thread," page 153, on the mechanics of handling the light line before attempting to use it.

GRANNICK'S BITTER APPLE

Invented in 1960 by a pharmacist, this substance has a multitude of uses, from applying it to a leash that your puppy has mistaken for a chew toy to applying it to your hand that your puppy has mistaken for a chew toy. Peppermint or cinnamon breath spray works, too.

A CRATE

Crates are useful for housebreaking and for containing dogs who like to explore their "Inner Decorator" while you're not home. I use either the all-enclosed Vari-Kennel or the fold-up wire crate from Midwest Homes for Pets. For dogs or puppies with claustrophobia issues, you can use an exercise pen (basically a portable crate without the top), also available from Midwest Homes for Pets.

A HUNGRY AND/OR MOTIVATED DOG!

If he's not hungry and motivated, *you* haven't primed him, and the training will be very difficult. Don't blame him!

CHAPTER 4

Puppy Training

One of the most common misconceptions has to be that you cannot train a dog before the age of six months. That falsehood needs to be dispelled this instant.

Attention Puppy Owners! You can actually start training at eight weeks!

There. I feel much better now.

Most professionals know that at eight weeks a puppy is a virtual training sponge! Those trainers (myself included) have always taken advantage of this time of maximum dependency and minimum ego to teach such basics as "sit," "come," and "down," just to name a few. Even the skills expected of our adults dogs (e.g., running through tunnels and retrieving metal objects) are easier if the concept has been at least introduced early. Just as kids are best taught foreign languages when they're very young, dogs have a leg up on learning if you ignore conventional wisdom and don't wait.

If you're still skeptical about the value of trying to train your puppy, ask yourself this:

Is your puppy old enough to get hit by a car?

If you answered yes, then you've got a puppy that needs

training. Don't be lulled into the false comfort of the "But he's always on a leash" excuse—he is only until he isn't! He could break free, someone could let go of the leash. That's what we mean by accidents, and accidents do happen.

Motivation is easy to come by. Most puppies are bottomless pits for food motivation. Because they've just been parted from the familiar faces of their puppy siblings, they also want to be close to someone. As they haven't yet had a chance to invent any bad habits, they'll be keen to learn some fun games. (Either you teach them something, or they'll pick up something in the street, which, in all likelihood, you won't like.) Hmmm, let's put all this another way: The puppy is a dog who is hungry, lonely, and bored. Bingo! (If you're not sharing the revelation, get with the program, you chapter skipper, you!) Puppydom is the optimal life stage for dog training! If this logic is lost on you, put yourself in a hard sit and reread "Stacking the Biscuits in Your Favor" on page 28.

Puppy training also makes the typing part of training simpler. All dogs are emphatically different, but, like human babies, puppies as a group have many more traits in common than do adults. The bond that's created between trainer and dog is very strong, but it's especially strong when you train a puppy, when eagerness to please is most pronounced. How silly not to take advantage of the "What can I do for you?" stage of development and wait for the "Huh, what do you know anyway?" stage. It's like waiting to potty-train a teenager. At six months your dog will cease to "puppy" after you with adoring eyes and begin to run around the house looking for things to destroy. Do I have your vote yet?

THINGS EVERY PUPPY MUST LEARN

The following are absolute musts if you don't want the puppy police sent to your house to remove the dog and replace it with a Betta fish.

Teach Your Puppy to Wear a Leash and Collar

Hugely important! If the puppy pitches a fit over a collar and leash, how will you ever train him? I've seen it in class more times than I care to remember. Someone brings a six-month-old puppy bucking and flailing at the end of a lead. The owner proudly tells me it's the first time the puppy has ever worn a leash and collar. Actually it's often the first time the owner has ever been able to catch him, having allowed the puppy free run of his or her property (which, under questioning, the owner admits is unfenced). Assuming you don't enjoy hysteria, teach your puppy to accept a leash and collar before teaching commands such as "sit" and "down."

Most puppies acclimate with reasonable ease to the buckle collar. In the odd case, you may observe a determination to scratch it off, but this is nothing compared with the more prevalent reaction to the dreaded leash. To accustom him to the latter, I introduce the leash to the puppy at the earliest possible moment by letting him, under my supervision, walk around the house dragging behind him a leash attached to his collar. The puppy will inevitably step on it, impeding his progress, and thus learn to accept the tugging sensation on his collar. There are dogs who can drag an SUV behind them without fuss, and then there are dogs who, at the slightest tug, will howl as if chased by the Hounds of Hell. For the tug-sensitive puppy, you will need a bit of bribery to alleviate the mainly psychological reaction. Here are some suggestions.

I'm Hysterical! I'm Hysterical! Now I'm Wet and Hysterical! (to paraphrase Mel Brooks's The Producers)

Remember that scene in the 1968 movie version of *The Producers* in which Zero Mostel throws water on a totally hysterical Gene Wilder? Of course it doesn't help. He's now wet *and* hysterical. I see the same dynamic a lot with dog owners. The dog is pitching a fit, and the owner gets upset and starts ranting himself. The unnerving tones serve only to upset the puppy more, as well as make an embarrassing spectacle of human frustration. Simply put, a bad situation made even worse. Try this: First, take off that leash. (If a leash with a ten-pound bolt was on your two-pound dog, you are in *so* much trouble for not reading Chapter 3 about equipment!) Take a nice long shoelace, and, in a confined area where you can fully supervise, let him drag around the lace attached to the collar. Big and small dogs alike will benefit from this. It takes some of the weight off their necks while still acclimating them to the pulling sensation. Play with your puppy, reward him with dog cookies, and generally try to provide him with as much fun as you can while he has the shoelace on. He will incrementally become used to the sensation and equate it with pleasure.

Do I hear the sounds of leather munching? For those dogs that have either identified the leash or shoelace as a chew toy or have managed to remove the offending appendage with their teeth (I said, supervise them!) you may spray, or soak, the shoelace in Grannick's Bitter Apple. If your puppy *likes* Bitter Apple, feel free to experiment with Tabasco, lemon juice, or whatever nontoxic sourpusser you may have. I don't have to tell you to apply the deterrent before you attach the lace (or *leash*!) to the collar, do I? After a few days of shoelace dragging, your puppy will be ready to learn how to walk on his leash.

Teaching Your Puppy to Walk on a Leash

The aim is for you to walk *him,* not vice versa (which, chances are, he's already mastered). Making sure, as always, that your puppy is in the mood to work (hungry, lonely, and/or bored) and that you have a wonderful food or toy lure in your pocket, let's begin!

1. In a quiet, distraction-free environment, show the puppy your lure—maybe even let him have a nibble (or a tug, if it's a toy) to pique his interest.
2. Walking slowly backward with the lure inches from your puppy's nose, see if you can get him to follow you as you back up. If he puts on the brakes, don't worry;

keep backing up and praising. After he's taken two steps toward you, reward and release. Repeat. If your puppy readily follows you, go ten steps before you reward. When he seems reliable at ten, you may proceed to step 3.

3. Start backing up as before, but now pivot left so that you and the puppy are facing the direction in which you were just backing up. He should now be on your left side. The food should be directly over his nose, and your hand should be held even with the seam of your pants. All the while praise the puppy in a very animated and upbeat voice.

When your puppy is walking next to you without fuss or fighting, you're ready for the "Teaching 'Let's Go'" section on page 156.

If Your Puppy Is (Still!) Pitching a Major Fit

A physically and mentally healthy puppy should eventually acclimate to walking on a leash, assuming that you are not being abusive and have taken your time to do steps 1–3 methodically. If he hasn't gotten used to the leash, let's back up (metaphorically this time). When your puppy has his tantrums, are you or have you ever been in the habit of trying to pacify him with sweet nothings? ("Oh, sweetie, come on, come on, come on, come on.") How about picking him up and holding him? Both responses work against his learning how to walk on a leash. Lesson learned: A little grousing and you're off the hook, literally. Dogs take the cues from you; change your behavior, and your puppy's will almost certainly change, too. Instead of stopping during a fit, continue walking and speaking in a pleasant tone. Remember to praise and reward even one or two nonresistant steps. Soon these will multiply and become a whole walk!

Teaching Your Puppy to Be Comfortable with Being Handled

This is so important it should be enshrined in a book of its own. Repeat after me, "Puppies MUST learn to accept being handled by the family and strangers!"

Some definition: "Handling" is the examination of the various body parts of your puppy. Tummy rubs and head pats are forms of affection, but they don't count as handling. Handling is much more invasive, and something a dog must learn to tolerate from whoever needs to handle him. It's not a tolerance that comes automatically (are *you* ticklish?), but it's important in facilitating grooming chores such as brushing, ear and teeth cleaning, and nail clipping. It's even more vital if your dog is injured. In the case of, say, a hurt paw, "convenient" is not the word to describe the value of a dog willing to sit still while you look between his pads for a piece of glass. Your dog will learn to accept (though not necessarily to enjoy) invasion of his privacy without flailing, biting, or bucking only *if* you teach him what is expected.

Note: Even though I'm using the word "puppy" in these examples, this training works for (and is imperative for!) dogs of all ages. And while you'll obviously exert a bit more physical energy convincing your four-year-old Great Dane to assume the "settle" position, it is truly a worthwhile endeavor.

Teaching "Settle"

"Settle" is the command I use as I'm moving the puppy into one of the two positions used for examinations. The positions are side (figure 1) or back (figure 2).

For the side position, start seated on the floor, back against the wall or a couch. That way, if you're in for a battle, at least you have rear support. Gently place the puppy on his side, his legs pointing away from you while you are saying, "Settle." When he is on the ground, gently grasp the scruff of his neck with your left hand and begin your examinations with your right.

If you're settling him on his back (particularly useful for

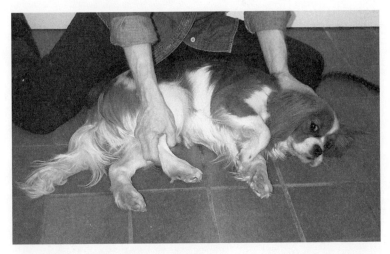

Figure 1. Settle position on side.

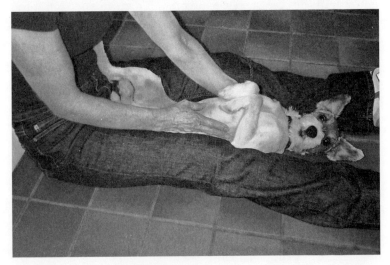

Figure 2. Settle position on back.

clipping nails), your legs should be straight out in front of you. Lift your puppy up, and, turning him spine-down, place him between your legs (figure 3). *Gently* use your legs as a vise if he resists staying on his back.

With your puppy in a settle position, you may begin the exam. This is just a drill. It includes touching between his toes (dogs have very sensitive feet), touching inside his ears, looking at his teeth and, occasionally, petting him. Notice I said

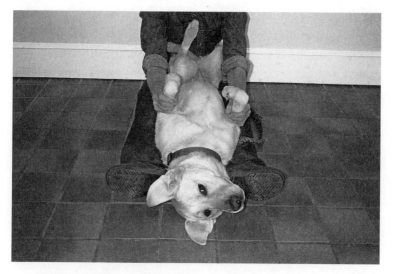

Figure 3. Settle position, large dog version.

"occasionally." This is not a massage! With a puppy who is being very calm and quiet you can, in an equally calm and quiet voice, praise him. If at any point your puppy tries to get up or struggle, give him a firm shake by the scruff and repeat, "Settle," in a calm voice. Yes, you can reach his scruff even if he's upside down! If you have a biter, you can give him a tiny squirt of Grannick's Bitter Apple or peppermint breath spray (see page 42) in the mouth before telling him again to settle. When he does "settle" (lying quietly without a struggle), praise him in a calm, soothing voice. After you're finished examining him, tell him, "Okay," in a flat, unanimated voice and let him stand up. Don't have a party and start cheering as soon as he's on his feet and bouncing—he will only form the impression that escaping was the point of the exercise! Wait a few minutes and begin again. The second time you attempt this exercise, your puppy may be more resistant to lying down, because, like a wrestler, he's invented some counter-moves. Be persistent and make him settle. (When he's seventy pounds heavier, you'll be glad you took the time to do this now!) With practice, he'll become more tolerant of being put in a settle position; then you can start making your probes more invasive. At this point I would introduce a nail clipper to the exercise; just tap the top of each nail with it. All puppies should learn to let their owners clip their nails—whether a groomer will be doing it later or not! Here's the objective: Your puppy can keep no area of his body "off-limits" to you. Privacy advocates may object, but sorry—this is a dog's life. What about the dog who has had an injury or surgery and you have to clean the affected area and put medicine on it? Three times a day? Even when you're tired? You've paid for the whole dog, nose to tail, and you should be able to handle him wherever and whenever necessary. For the ear exam practice drill you can now swipe the inside of the ear with a cotton ball. Resistance at any point is to be met by a firm shake of the scruff and the word "settle" before resuming.

Although hardly a party-trick order such as "roll over," "settle" is an incredibly important command. If you cannot convince your dog that you're allowed to examine him as you will, you face a lifetime of escalating power-sharing struggles. Consider it a diagnostic: A dog who won't let you touch his feet will certainly not give you 100 percent commitment in training, either. (If you haven't done this homework and practiced on a whole, healthy dog, you're going to have to introduce him to this experience at a moment of urgency in an area on his body where he least wants you to go, just when he's feeling his worst. Under such circumstances you may want to invest in some falconry gloves and invite the neighbors over to help you hold him down.)

Beware of Those Who Bite the Hand That Feeds Them

I'd say about 5 percent of the dogs I see attempt to vote with their teeth on my curriculum; 4.5 percent, once corrected, do catch on; and .5 percent are a little tougher. In twenty years of seeing thousands of dogs, I've seen only three so pathologically aggressive that they needed to be destroyed. The problem with pathologically aggressive dogs is that some of them can be taught nice manners—"sit"; "wait"; even "come"—but when they hit that red zone, that rage, they're gone. Envision it as a seizure of sorts, which, when they enter this state, puts them in a place where you temporarily can't reach them. I know, there are those well-meaning souls who say that no animal need be destroyed. But this is not the place for debate, and you bought the book for my advice. Here it is: I know that there are dogs out there who are going to take the face off someone's beautiful grandchild because someone's either in denial or hasn't recognized the signs. If aggression surfaces, no matter how mild, you must take off your rose-colored glasses and bring in a professional trainer to make this call. There are some problems that are too complicated or formidable for the amateur to deal with. One of the values of a good training program is that it teaches you to identify such problems. At this moment, I have a huge dead tree in my yard. A part of me naturally believes it would be a very simple matter to handle myself—I do have a power saw, after all. My better judgment, however, tells me that a professional will know for certain how to fell the tree without hitting my house, the neighbors', or the power lines. Anything I urge you to try in this book is within a reasonable margin for error. Teeth and growling require a professional trainer to be at your side.

The Comfort of Strangers

Once your puppy has received all required vaccinations, you can take him new places and start teaching him that people are great fun to be around. Shyness toward unknown humans will always be a chink in the armor of any good training.

Four on the Floor

Although it's lovely to hold a puppy, too much time aloft will inadvertently condition him always to expect humans to meet him on those terms—face-to-face. It also leads to a chronic jumper, which you'll regret when the puppy is no longer "pick-upable!"

Speak Softly and Wear Rubber Shoes

Those who greet your puppy should be asked to come down to his level and address him in soft, calm tones. Hypereffusive and high-pitched greetings can condition your puppy to become overly excited by people; that, too, can lead to a chronic jumper. If your puppy is a shy or nervous type, over-the-top greetings can lead to nervous peeing, never a crowd-pleaser.

"I Sit for Strangers!"

Always have a food reward on hand when you take a puppy out. When a new person approaches, hand him a dog treat to offer your puppy. If your puppy knows how to sit for a treat, tell the person to show the treat to the puppy and ask for the sit. If your puppy learns that sitting for strangers gains him a treat, he will abandon (or never start) becoming a chronic jumper. For puppies who are more inclined to work for a toy or a "scritch," substitute that for the food.

Shy? You're FINE!

If you have a nervous or shy puppy, *never* use the "poor puppy" tone of voice, as in, "Ohh, baby boy, it's okay, whatza-matter with Mommie's wittle bay-bee?" Apart from inciting others to slap you, this only adds to the inventory of sounds the dog can't understand—in general, the smaller and more consistent the vocabulary you employ, the better chance your dog will keep his orders straight. Mollycoddling only confirms his irrational fear of whatever has spooked him. Better to say, "You're fine—let's go!" in an upbeat, confident tone. Familiar words, reassuring tone.

Truly fearful dogs will do much better if people approach without making eye contact initially, and perhaps refrain from speaking to them for a few minutes. If someone assaulted *you* with, "Ohh, my GAWD what a cute puppy, my husband's gotta see him. HARR-OLLD, come see this cute puppy. Draco, honey, stop trying to pull the puppy's tail. HARR-OLLD, I said, get ovah heah!!!" you'd probably freak out, too. Even the most grounded puppy finds such ebullience unbearably overstimu-lating. So while I do generally counsel exposing puppies to all aspects of life (the good, the bad, and the flamboyant), when you see it coming, there's no reason not to run as if from the Plague.

If you encounter such a situation, do not go into the "It's okay, puppy-wuppy" monologue.

Do politely explain to these well-meaning sociopaths that you left your stove on and have to run home. Walk the puppy back to the car, pop him into his crate, and breath a sigh of relief.

On the Road Again

When in transit, you *must* have that puppy in a crate. Don't give me the "I'm only going a few minutes away!" routine. You buckle up in the car, right? Your kids buckle up, right? If you answered no to either of those questions, you may not have outgrown your own Rebel-Without-a-Cause stage, and probably require a different sort of professional. Grow up, buckle up, and secure that dog. If your car is struck, your dog could become a projectile, dangerous to himself and to passengers. One of my students was in a serious car accident and her dog, only slightly injured, became very protective and wouldn't let the EMTs near her. They had to waste valuable time waiting for the Animal Control unit before they could administer medical treatment! Dogs can also react unpredictably to the stimuli of the great wide world. What if you're driving and your dog spots something that inspires him to bound across the steering wheel? Small dogs can cause big problems down among the pedals. Many a freak accident involving a loose dog could have been prevented by the use of a crate or a doggie seat belt (yes, they have them!).

Home Alone

Learning to stay home alone is as important a training experience as learning to go out. As a corollary to a rule you already have, you aren't allowed to say, "It's okay, pookie-woozie. Mommie's going out, but it's okay. I'll be back. Ohh, poor thing!" Dogs can sniff out impending doom and can be even more paranoid than humans.

A special toy—a stuffed Kong toy, a little plush animal, whatever she loves best—should be designated as one that your puppy never gets to play with except when she's home alone. This eases the transition to solitary confinement. Put the toy in the crate with her, close the door, and in your best casual voice say, "See you later," then pick up your keys and leave. Save the uncontrollable sobbing for when you have cleared the driveway.

Puppy Recalls

This is a great game and the foundation for the basic "come when called" command. When you begin training, play it at least once a day, more often if possible. You cannot do too many puppy recalls!

As with all training, start with a hungry, lonely, and/or bored puppy. Take everyone who wants to play into a small room with the door closed. Give each person a handful of treats. Make sure these are *great* treats, not just some sorry dry biscuits that will take twenty minutes to chew. If your puppy is motivated enough by toys or by playing with you, that should serve. Since, however, most puppies are "walking stomachs," motivating with food rarely fails.

As you hold the puppy by the collar (the leash attached, but not to be used unless he tries to run away), ask everyone to be seated and have one person call the dog. DO NOT use the command "here," as we are saving that for the formal recall. Instead, try something like "Pookie, come, pup, pup, pup!" I know what you're saying: "That's not a command, that's inflammatory blather!" Yes and no. The goal of this exercise is to get the puppy worked into such a frenzy that he practically drags the person holding the collar across the room just to get to the caller. Stick to verbal incitement at first. Once that succeeds, you can also clap, tap the floor—anything to maximize his urge to run to the caller. When the frenzy has peaked, the holder releases the collar. As the puppy runs to the caller, he should praise the puppy in an animated voice, the praise reaching a climax when he arrives, at which point he is also rewarded with the food treat. After this homecoming drama subsides, the next person calls the puppy, with the last caller now holding the collar. Continue in this manner until everyone has had a turn *or* until the puppy starts to look tired. At the first sign of fatigue, stop the game and put the puppy away. You always want to stop training while a dog still wants to do more.

You can increase the size of the circle and the room in which the game is played. If you try this outdoors, however, the leash is especially important. This game makes for very good conditioning throughout puppyhood to reinforce the fun and pleasure of coming to you. By playing recalls when your dog is young, you'll make the eventual teaching of the formal "come" command much easier.

Teach Your Puppy Some Basic Commands

Now you may go to the "Teaching 'Sit' " (page 68) and "Teaching 'Down' " (page 102) sections and start teaching your puppy these important behaviors that many adult dogs haven't mastered. Do everything described up until you reach the correction stage for each behavior. Adding corrections must wait until the puppy has reached the age of four months, and so must teaching the "wait" command. The only exception to the no-corrections-before-four-months rule is the "come"command, in the teaching of which I use a "pop" correction on dogs as young as twelve weeks. Whether it's okay to teach the command with correction, of course, is based on whether you've spent lots of time doing recalls, have taught the "here" command thoroughly, and are sure that the puppy understands the exercise before he is corrected. Trained methodically, even a young puppy can learn to come when called.

HOUSEBREAKING

Many of you may have turned to this section first, having bought the book for a related emergency. Believe me, I understand: Housebreaking noncompliance is the number-one problem I'm asked to fix. Yesterday isn't quick enough when "number one" and "number two" are gracing your bare floors or precious rugs. It's a delicate subject that frays more nerves than any other aspect of dog ownership. Even the term, "housebreaking," suggests a bruising contest of wills. Blessed are the peacemakers. Let's housebreak your puppy!

I STRONGLY advocate the use of a crate for housebreaking a puppy or even an older dog. I caution against paper training, the practice of first teaching the dog to do his business on paper in the house, before "breaking" it to him that the house is no longer acceptable and his only bathroom is the great outdoors. I don't advocate paper training because I hate to unteach something I've taught, especially since there is no good reason not to teach from the outset the behavior you ultimately desire. This line of thinking is not to imply a shortcut. Housebreaking requires substantial time and effort on your part. You'll have to go outside through rain and sleet and snow and maybe even during the Oscars. Nature does not keep regular hours, and for a kicker, sometimes the puppy won't want to go and you'll have to make him. You may be late to the party and may have to leave said party early. While you're wondering whether it's you or the dog who's being "broken," bear in mind that the problem doesn't last forever. Though there will be other challenges in having a dog, none will test your humanity like this one.

As I see it, there are four major issues in housebreaking—food, cleanup, crate, and schedule.

The Food

The most useful thing you'll ever learn about housebreaking—and I am not being facetious: DON'T GIVE YOUR DOG A PUPPY FOOD HIGH IN FIBER! A lot of puppy foods are incomprehensibly overloaded with fiber, which may explain why the manufacturers suggest feeding a puppy twenty-two cups a day. I'm not plugging any particular brand here (no endorsement deals, alas!) but I find that the food stocked only in pet stores and unavailable in supermarkets is generally better. That said, I was walking through the local Shop Rite this week and saw a huge high-end dog-food display in the pet aisle. Some great dog foods are now finding their way into supermarkets. Your vet can suggest one.

I don't recommend those foul-smelling canned foods or any semi-moist variety that promises to stay "mushy and beefy." In fact, beef is usually the last thing a lab analysis will reveal in those sludgy canned mixtures laden with unspeakable animal byproducts and vile chemicals. Dogs react adversely to chemicals and excess sugar, just as people do. For your own quality of life, as well as the dog's, buy a high-quality dry food with moderate fiber content. (Check the label; personally, my dogs do well with a fiber content of about 5 percent. Canned foods tend to give them loose stools.) You'll feed less of it and have less cleanup. (Thought you'd like that.) You'll also facilitate housebreaking if you feed your puppy *carefully measured* meals at approximately the same time each day. Free feeding leads to free pooping! If he doesn't finish his food in twenty minutes, pick up what's left and serve it at the next meal. Just as your dog must learn that "going potty" means waiting for "potty time," he needs to expect to eat only when a meal is served. (Goes for kids, too.)

The Crate

In my experience, housebreaking problems are as common as "home alone" problems—damage done when your dog is unsupervised in the house. All can be eliminated with the use of the crate, if only more people would realize that crating is not cruel or unusual punishment. In fact, it's no kind of punishment at all (stop projecting!). Being crated approximates being in a den, the space in which dogs in the wild state slept for thousands of years. Wild dogs still exist and still sleep in dens. The domesticated dog retains the den instinct, which is why the use of a crate is so effective in housebreaking. Normally, a dog will not foul his den.* In days before domestication, when dogs were predators, they needed a safe place not

---

*Unfortunately, some dogs will use their crate as a Port-A-John. Usually these puppies are either being overfed, kept in a crate for too long, or kept in too

only to get their z's but to rear their young. If they used the den as a potty, natural enemies would have picked up the scent and preyed on the doggie young or sick. Thus, dogs today are programmed to do their utmost to avoid soiling their sleeping quarters.

Practically speaking, a crated dog might try to create a cordon sanitaire. To avoid this, his crate must be small enough that it becomes impractical to designate one end as a bedroom and one end as a bathroom. A crate should be just large enough that the puppy/dog can stand up and turn around. Anything smaller is unkind; anything larger invites unwelcome interior design. There are two main types of crates: wire crates and airline crates. Wire crates offer a better view and better ventilation than airline crates, which mostly are made of tough plastic and vented at both ends. If you purchase a wire crate, be sure to get one that can fold down like a suitcase. (Even if you don't plan on taking it anywhere, this option will prove a blessing one day. The other type of wire crate is less expensive but requires more mechanical skill to assemble than most of us possess. You have to line up the four side panels and then drop a metal post down through the channel—in the panel—at the corners. If you've done this correctly, then you're a member of Mensa, so you get to put the wire top on. If you've done it incorrectly, you're in the majority. Go find a few friends and promise them anything if they're willing to help you out.) Airline crates are generally less expensive, can be used to ship a dog (to Siberia if necessary!), and have the added virtue of containing any accidents or shedding. Crates can cost

---

big a crate. Or perhaps they came from a pet shop or puppy mill, where there was no choice but to go to the bathroom in the crate they lived in!

If you believe the problem may be overfeeding, try reducing the amount of food, or switching to a brand of higher quality. Keep in mind that "too long" is subjective. Your puppy is okay for three hours, your neighbor's can go for four. If the crate is too large, section it off. As for those pet-store puppies, they need extra attention, which may include taking them out twice as often as you would a normally potty-trained puppy. In any event, a thorough veterinary exam is the most reliable way to diagnose a physical problem that could be causing difficulty in housebreaking your puppy.

anywhere from thirty to two hundred dollars or more; you can generally get the best price using dog-supply catalogs. If you have a puppy that will grow into a large dog, and you don't want to buy two crates, buy a large one and block off the back section of the crate with a piece of plywood. Some companies sell "crate dividers" just for that purpose. You can move or remove a divider as the puppy grows larger.

Most important of all: *The crate must never be used as punishment!* If the crate is to serve your purposes, the dog must see it as he's naturally programmed to see it: his special place where he is safe and happy. Putting him in there when he does wrong works against his hardwiring. Many breeders crate-train their puppies from the time they leave the whelping box. If you are purchasing from a breeder (as I strongly recommend you do), ask if the puppy has been introduced to the crate. Before bringing the puppy home, take a towel or small blanket and ask the breeder to put it in the whelping box with the puppies. The cloth will then be permeated with the mother/litter scent and will do much to ease those first few nights that we all dread.

THE SCHEDULE

From the moment your puppy arrives home, he should always be crated under the following circumstances:

- **He is napping.**
  One minute you're playing with him; the next, he's crashed out on the floor, sound asleep. This high-energy little one can get spent before he knows it. When this happens, pick him up, take him to his crate (aka his bedroom), and close the door. He needs to get used to sleeping in the crate. When he's older and feels sleepy, he'll go lie down in it all by himself. Again, if the dog is of a breed that typically exceeds twenty pounds in adulthood, one day you'll be grateful you trained him in puppyhood.

- **It's nighttime.**

  I presume you like to sleep at night and don't want your house redecorated nocturnally in "Country Cocker Spaniel"?

- **It's mealtime.**

  Trust me, this is the best place for the puppy when he's eating. This teaches him to focus on his food rather than on what is going on around him, a trait that you will want to harness in training. Toddlers use a high chair; dogs use a crate.

- **You are too busy for active supervision.**

  You might be busy, or the dog may be tired or your entire family has the flu. If at a given moment you can't *watch the puppy*—and I mean in the same room, watching him, not the TV!—a little effort to crate him is better than a bigger effort to clean up after him. Besides, every opportunity your puppy has to make a mistake in the house only sets back your housebreaking.

Punching the Potty "Time Clock"

In his crate your puppy can hold it in for a few hours, but do not overtax his patience, or his kidneys. When not crated, your puppy will need to go outside every twenty to thirty minutes. This is nothing to be lax about. Only by going out this frequently will he receive enough object lessons in the difference between right (outdoor elimination) and wrong (relieving himself in your slippers). Puppies are naturally without decorum, and they are poor prognosticators of their own bodily processes. An adult dog thinks, "Uh-oh, I've got that feeling. I'd better get someone to let me out!" A puppy, however, says, "Uh-oh, I've got a funny feeling—ahhhh, that's better!" So you have to anticipate the need and accustom the puppy to making the right choice. If you really need it spelled out, here's a "Day in the Life" of one of my current puppy students and his owner. Names have been changed to protect the exhausted.

A Day in the Life of "Joe" and Puppy "Maxie"

- Maxie starts barking at 5:00 a.m. Joe stumbles out of bed, cracks his shin on the door, and lumbers down the stairs. He takes Maxie out of the crate, attaches the leash, picks Maxie up, and carries him outside. But he doesn't talk to him! (I know, at 5:00 a.m. who talks? Just like breakfast with the Missus. Seriously, though, if you're a chipper riser, you'll have to restrain yourself and be silent with the puppy.)

- Joe puts Maxie down in his designated potty area (DPA), taking care that it is the same spot every time. Then Joe gives the "go to the bathroom" command. This can be anything you like, so long as it's consistent—"Hurry up"; "You go, boy"; "Let it whip!"—anything you don't mind saying in front of strangers, which may eliminate "Go poo-poos"; "Make a winkie"; "Number one, please"; and my personal favorite, "Leave us a present!" Joe, a regular guy, favors "Hurry up!"

- Maxie pees and then after a while he poops. Actually, this is speculation: Joe was cheating, trying to catch some extra shut-eye while standing. But Maxie is now frolicking about, so Joe deduces that the dog has relieved himself of all burdens. They walk back toward the house, and halfway across the lawn Joe steps in a lustrous, fresh pile of puppy poop. "I guess I guessed right!" Some might be put out, but Joe with his pet-stained carpet, takes it in stride. "Hey, at least I'm wearing slippers this time!"

- Back in the house Joe puts his puppy back into the crate and feeds him a carefully measured breakfast. Maxie happily gobbles it up—in a world-record time of thirty-two seconds!

- Now Joe takes him from the crate for a little supervised "out" time in the barricaded kitchen. Free run of the house is unthinkable until the housebreaking is accomplished. Joe sets his microwave timer for thirty minutes to remind himself about Maxie's next walk.

- Twenty-five minutes later the puppy is sniffing and walking in circles near his feet. Recognizing this as a sign, Joe picks him up, attaches the leash, and bolts out the back door. Joe airlifts Maxie to the DPA, but before he can say, "Hurry up," Maxie is in a squat and watering the grass. Close call. Joe praises Maxie (and himself for being so alert to his puppy's needs); they go back into the house.

- A few minutes later, Joe smells trouble. He turns around to see Maxie squatting and pooping. He says, "Ah-ah!" in a mildly agitated voice (containing his horror), quickly scoops Maxie up, and races to the DPA. Joe puts Maxie in position and praises him for being in the right place (albeit at the wrong time). He waits a few minutes, then returns to the house. Joe remembers my counsel to never, never, never yell at his puppy for making a mistake in the house. He knows that to vent his frustrations would only succeed in scaring Maxie, perhaps promoting submissive urination or, worse, a dog who goes into hiding when he goes to the bathroom—location unknown. Trust me, finding it later is worse than seeing the deed happen in real time.

- Joe goes back inside and, gently, quietly, puts Maxie in his crate for some quiet time. Crucially, this period in the crate isn't punishment for his having an accident in the house. If it were, getting Maxie in there would be a harder and harder task. Maxie likes his crate and enjoys the security of quiet time, especially following a morning of mixed results. True, when Joe first crated Maxie, the experience was more like "screaming and crying and barking time." I told him to cover Maxie's crate with a sheet, and that did the trick. Alternatively, you can move the crate to a quieter room, away from all the domestic commotion.

Operation: Cleanup

Joe's next job, alas, is to clean up the poop. He uses one of those special enzyme-digesting cleaners such as Nature's Miracle. This thoroughly deodorizes the spot, which is important, since dogs, drawn by scent, will naturally go to the same spot to do their business, no matter how wrong that spot may be. (When you see them sniffing outside, they are looking either for their own calling card or that of others; detecting a scent, they will usually pee directly over it, marking, or remarking, the spot as their own.)

If your puppy is very young, or just not "getting it" when it comes to housebreaking, try this: Take the poop outside and put it down on the DPA. It will be a lesson to your puppy, who won't know he didn't put it there himself. In the case of pee, blot it up with an old towel, and put that out on the DPA.

Don't use anything with ammonia in it to clean up puppy accidents. Ammonia is a component of urine, and "pine-scented" cleansers smell like pine and urine to your dog, misleading him to believe that he has found the sweet spot. Try a little diluted bleach or, for a less toxic approach, a little diluted white vinegar on your floor. In fact, keep in mind the canine's powerful sense of smell, and banish ammonia-based cleaners altogether until your puppy is totally housebroken—if you don't want your spick-and-span house to be used as a toilet.

- By the time the kitchen is clean, Joe notices that an hour has passed. Maxie must answer the call of nature. To the DPA!
- Fast-forward through hourly outdoor potty breaks until lunch, which is the same as breakfast. Joe keeps Maxie in

the crate until he's done eating (if he's not done in twenty minutes, the rest is saved for dinner). Then, it's outside for the postprandial potty.

- Fast-forward through various play sessions, potty breaks, inside (oops!) and outside. Joe's main rule is: If the puppy is out of the crate, then he has to be confined to a small area of the house (such as the kitchen) and taken outside every twenty to thirty minutes. If Maxie is in his crate, he can hold it for a few hours, as long as he was taken out *just before* being crated and taken out immediately upon Joe's return. Remember that a puppy with an emptied bowel and bladder is going to reward *you* with an empty crate when you return home.
- Five p.m. Dinnertime. See earlier regarding breakfast and lunch.
- Maxie gets no food after 5:30 and no water after 6:00 p.m. This insures an empty bowel and bladder by bedtime, so Joe (and Maxie) can sleep through the night. (For adult dogs, no such restrictions will apply.)
- Joe's last walk with Maxie is between ten and eleven p.m. Maxie used to go in the middle of the night but only during his first few nights of housebreaking.

If your puppy still needs to relieve himself in the middle of the night after a week or two on such a schedule, there could be some "weak links" in the housebreaking team. Maybe someone is sneaking food or water to the puppy. If there are no culprits, rest assured that a physically healthy puppy *will* outgrow this stage.

Hey! Is Joe a Retired Multimillionaire or a Trustafarian?!

I can hear some of you now, saying, "Whoa! I work nine to five. How am I supposed to take my puppy outside that much?" Hmm, how can I put this gently? . . . *"What were you thinking when you got a puppy?!"* In some ways the first six months of a puppy's life can be as time-consuming as an infant's first six months. Young dogs need constant care and supervision, not to mention training. If you have a puppy, you need to take account of these realities. (Next time, you may want to consider adopting a one-year-old dog, and avoid the housebreaking Sturm und Drang.)

Find yourself a reliable dog caretaker, either by referral, through your vet, or in your local paper. You'll need someone who can come in to walk and play with your puppy every three hours—at minimum! As the puppy hits four and five months of age, you can extend the interval between caretaking activities to four hours, but at that point you may want to consider a puppy day-care center (yes, they have them), which can furnish not only the care and attention she needs but also socialization. First, there were latch-key kids; now, there are latch-key dogs. Fortunately, your options are much greater than they were ten years ago. Dogs who sit home alone crated all day until night cannot be blamed for using your couch as an arts-and-crafts project when let out!

THE BOTTOM LINE

Accept the fact that, during the training stages, your puppy will occasionally regress and make mistakes even after you think she is housebroken. As with most training failures, the mishap is usually the result of humans failing to read the signs. Do not despair—if you have children, you know that baby stages mean baby steps, and things can only get easier—until, of course, they really get difficult once your darling is no longer a baby. If you're a glutton for punishment, skip now to "Top Ten Behavior Problems Frequently Used as Temporary Insanity Pleas" (page 184) for a menu of the priceless experiences to come.

CHAPTER 5

Basic Commands

TEACHING "SIT"

The definition of a perfect sit: The handler (speaking in a normal-level but firm tone of voice) says "[Dog's name], sit." The dog, no matter what he is doing, immediately sits, bringing his hind feet up behind his front legs. The handler never repeats the command, snaps his fingers, raises his voice, bends at the waist, or engages in any manner of contortion.

Ripley's Believe It or Not? No, this scenario involves an average trainer with an average dog. Since, however, "sit" is the first command you will teach your dog using my method, beginning the instruction is bound to be a momentous occasion for both of you. It will mark the first step in teaching your dog not only how to sit, but how to learn! After that, there's almost no end to how many things you can teach him to do. But you must begin with a *total understanding* of teaching, rewarding, correcting, and distracting your dog, and how these relate to one another. Even more than the strategies for teaching individual commands, this chapter aims to impart that total understanding to you. Read it through at least once before attempting to train. When you're sure you have a handle on all the pieces, the big picture will emerge, and you can attach that leash and get to work!

The Checklist

1. Make sure your dog is *ready to train*. Remember: "hungry, lonely, and/or bored"—ideally all three. Avoid the fool's errand of training a dog who isn't inspired to work.

2. Pick your motivator. If your dog is food motivated, the motivator must be something she can eat in three seconds or less. Longer than that, and the motivator becomes a distraction, and training time morphs into mealtime. You want just enough to be motivating (sure, your kid would wash the dishes for twenty bucks, but he'd also do it for two). Forget those super-size dog biscuits or tartar-controlling, chew-till-you-drop canine cookies that could break your toe if you dropped one of them from eye level onto your foot. You can use one of those commercial treats that remain mysteriously moist for years on end, or perhaps freeze-dried liver for dogs, but I've never seen anyone fail with nickel-sized slices of hot dogs (turkey or chicken) or cheese sticks (no, I don't have stock in Oscar Mayer or Kraft). For those who fear going down the road of people food, imagining, "Oh, yeah, she's just trying to create a problem so she can sell her next book, *My Fat Dog Just Ate the House*," get ahold of yourselves. This is no conspiracy to change your dog's position on the food chain; I'm just telling you what I've noticed that works. And don't worry that the dog will become addicted to people food—his only sense of that term is something that sits on your plate; he has no idea *all* your food tastes better than his.

   "Along came a spider": For a dog who turns on for toys, find the one that makes him go bonkers, and bring it out *only* for training. I have seen these supertoys range from the ordinary (tennis balls, tug bone) to the eccentric (a rubber chicken, a smelly old sock) to the "strictly for cats" (a spider puppet on strings). If the dog loves it, he will train. And by the way, if you happen on something that really works, make sure that you buy a few of them. The woman with the spider on a string drove her family bonkers trying to find a fresh one of the very same sort when the first spider was chewed up beyond recognition. Alternative brands of spider toys (yes, there's a whole industry of arachnids for play apparently) cut no ice with her dog.

3. Be sure your dog is wearing a collar and leash. (See pages 40–41 for advice about choosing this equipment.)

4. Train in a quiet, distraction-free area.

Some more preliminaries . . .

Assume the position: If your dog is small, you yourself may want to start out sitting or kneeling as you teach the "sit" and the "down" commands. That way you won't need a chiropractor to repair your locked-up lumbars. Eventually, no matter what size your dog is, you will train on your feet.

By any other name: Please note that in the very beginning phase of training I do not use the word "sit." I have found that people have a difficult time being quiet while the dog figures out things: "Waldo, sit. Sit, SIT! Come on, you can sit. Sit, whatsamatter with you? SIT, siddown, you can't have the cookie until you do a little sit." Imagine trying to learn how to do *anything* while listening to that! Once I get the dog to sit reliably for the motivator, then I insert the word "sit"—speaking it *only once*. Consider it a rule: one dog, one command! In general, the dog must learn a behavior before he learns what you choose to call it. So don't roll out the magic word until he's doing the sit perfectly. Only then can he make a clear connection between what you say and exactly what you expect him to do when he hears "sit."

Finally, before beginning, you need to understand the mechanics of a sit. From a standing position, a dog can sit in one of two ways. He can keep his hind legs in place and walk his forelegs back. I call this maneuver in which the dog rolls away from you a "rock-back sit." If you had been able to touch his nose when he was standing, you'd have to lean forward to reach it when he's in a rock-back sit. The other type of sit I call the tuck sit: With forelegs straight, he pulls his hind legs under himself, behind his forelegs. In the tuck sit, he is the same distance from you as when he was standing, and his head is high enough for you to reach his collar without lumbar support. That's the ticket! The tuck sit is what we are after.

Ready? Then let's begin!

Plan A: The Food/Toy Method
(For dogs with moderate to high food, toy, or play drive)

1. Show your motivator (we're going to use food in these examples). Let the dog know you have it. Let him smell it, lick it, or even have a little nibble.
2. Hold the food a few inches over his head, and do nothing (figure 4). Say nothing. Just wait.
   Keep waiting.

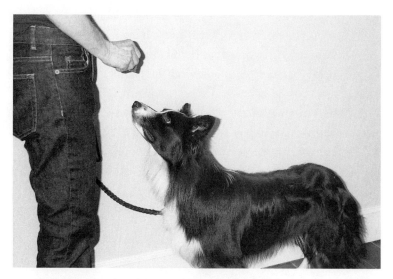

Figure 4. Showing the motivator and waiting.

3. Your dog is thinking: "How can I get the food?" He may be licking your hand, chewing on it, batting it with his nose or his paw, barking, or whining, but believe you me, he's thinking. Say nothing and wait some more. None of these gestures are going to get him what he wants. See what else he comes up with. There are dogs that will get bored and walk away and those that may become distracted. If either reaction occurs, step on the leash and refocus your dog on the food by putting it back in front of his nose again. A dog who *still* doesn't care either needs better food (go microwave some liver with garlic on it—really!), or isn't truly hungry, lonely, and/or bored. Go back to the section on building drives (page 10); you may need to adjust your evaluation or deprive him a bit more before training.

4. At some point it will occur to your dog to sit. Your response to this flash of inspiration should be "Yes!" followed immediately by the opening of your hand and the surrender of the food.* (By the way, an Akita named Lucy holds the record for forty-five minutes of prayerful staring at the hot dog first.) Giving the food is IMMEDIATELY followed by the release word "Okay."

5. If you're motivating with a toy, have a little play session with your dog, being sure to hold on to the toy! (He must never get what he wants until the exact moment he gives you what *you* want.) The length of playtime will depend on the type of dog you have. High-drive dogs may turn on with less play and more subdued praise, while the more laid-back types may need more toy playtime with more exuberant praise.

---

*Be sure that the food enters his mouth while he is still in a sit! The speed of your food delivery is vitally important!

IMPORTANT: After you say, "Yes!" and give the reward, you must say, "Okay," telling your dog to break the sit. That's the cue that his work here is done. Omitting this step, you will create a dog that sits (for rewards) and then gets up right away, which is almost as useless as not sitting in the first place. The "Yes!"–food reward–"Okay" sequence is happening so fast that only the final step allows the dog to see the end of the behavior and thus identify what exactly he has done right (in this case, a sit). He can do it again and again. In fact, he must break the sit to learn it. If you say, "Okay," and the dog doesn't move, you must physically (gently!) move him out of the sit and away from the release point. When I say, "Okay," I usually bend at the waist, move away from the dog (to encourage him to move, too), clap my hands, and generally get playful and happy. Of course, in the teaching stage you may be kneeling or sitting, so forget the "moving away from him" step. Don't worry; you'll get there soon enough! As we progress to "sit-wait," the reward will be delayed and eventually deleted, so there is not the promise of a treat but the understanding that if he doesn't obey, he will receive a correction. Where he was once obeying to win the thing desired, his motivation will change to avoiding the undesirable. Bait and switch? You got it.

As you repeat these steps note how quickly your dog abandons the wrong behaviors and offers you only the correct one.

If at this point you notice your dog favoring a rock-back sit, pressure the leash gently up and in toward you while he attempts the sit. This makes it harder for the dog to rock back, encouraging the tuck sit. Do this only when it seems clear to him that sitting is what you are after, and be careful not to apply so much pressure that he thinks you want him to stand.

6. Add your dog's name before the command "sit," as in "Tiger, sit." Hereafter, always ask for a sit by name. Always use a firm but pleasant voice and *never* repeat the command.

As always, train with focus for five to fifteen minutes, depending on perceived energy and work ethic, with a few breaks for playtime. (Sometimes dogs, especially puppies, need a brief mental break from training. Ten minutes to them is a long time!) And be sure to quit while your dog still wants to train more! The following day, start in the same location, but then move to another room. A command understood in the bedroom isn't necessarily recognized to be the same one in the living room. It will take a while for dogs to generalize and understand that the command means the same thing at any place or any time.

Once your dog is quickly sitting on command, those of you still sitting or kneeling on the floor need to progress to a more upright state (aka, standing!). If *you* were sitting when you taught your *dog* to sit, now is the time to go through the steps while kneeling. Next, try it standing up, but do bend at the waist. Finally, give the command while standing tall. Your dog may have some brief initial confusion about your new stature, but soon he'll be sitting no matter what position you happen to be in!

When your dog is obeying the command reliably, regardless of room or time of day or lunar cycle, it's time to take the show on the road. Move ahead to "Getting off the Chuck Wagon" (page 78), "Correcting the Sit" (page 80), and "A Distracting Situation" (page 84).

The Physical Approach

(Best for dogs with little to no food/toy/play drive.
Also good for those with low work ethic.)

Most of you will be quite satisfied with your results thus far. A few, however, may have your right arms in a tub of ice now. Assuming you are not a major-league pitcher, you probably did exactly as told and stood there for three hours while the dog stared at the hand with the food. There are various reasons for this, none of them especially comforting. Some dogs simply have modest or stunted food drives (they need to be ravenous before showing any interest). You can try cutting back food but ultimately you can't starve such a dog into training mode. Some, alas, have no connection with their owners, and some have their own ideas of a good time! Ask yourself whether you have been truly honest in evaluating your dog's lifestyle—remember Pookiebear! Go back and reread "Revealing and Boosting Your Dog's Prime Motivations" on page 10. See whether a little of the "Cold Withholder" doesn't make him want to earn that treat or toy or play session. If that doesn't work, we have a Plan B.

Plan B: The "Touchy-Feely" Method

So your dog won't take the bait—literally. That's all right. Although I prefer getting the dog to obey (sit, in this case) of his own volition, and thus to believe that what I want was his idea, not mine, there are times when the dog needs to be physically maneuvered into compliance and can learn well enough with that approach. Follow the checklist for Plan A, the Food/Toy Method, but with less emphasis on step 2. Also, *when using the Touchy-Feely Method, you must speak the command word from the outset* (otherwise the dog will be clueless as to why you are pulling on his collar, pressing down his rump, etc.).

• Stand (or sit or kneel) with your dog in front of you. The leash is on, but you are not holding it.

- Slip your hands under the collar, palms out, at 5:00 and 7:00. Close your fingers around the collar. You are now in "steering" position (figure 5).
- Tell your dog to sit, making sure you say his name first.
- Wait for a second or two (think, "One–one thousand").
- If there is no sit, use your arms to exert pressure up and toward your body. Maintain steady pressure as you try to

Figure 5. Holding collar in the "steering" position.

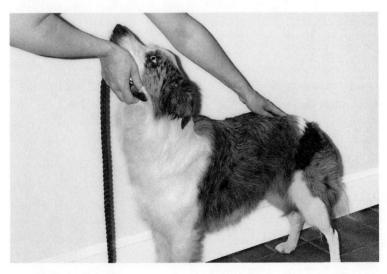

Figure 6. Reaching over to tuck rear into sit.

keep your elbows tucked in. Start with light pressure and increase gradually until you see that . . .

- The dog begins to drop his rear into a sit. Once he's in motion, be sure to let up on the pressure a bit so he can sit all the way down. As soon as his bottom hits the ground, say, "Yes!" Hold him there, and when you release, say, "Okay." Depending on your dog's personality type, the sit may be cause for a big celebration or some low-key praise. If your dog still won't sit, remove one of your hands from the "steering" position on the collar, reach over the dog, and tuck his back end into a sit while maintaining pressure with your other hand on the collar (figure 6).

- Repeat the process until you notice that the dog is sitting on command without collar pressure. Now you can let go of the collar and hold on to the leash. Hold it close to the snap, left hand over right. Your left hand is in a fist, thumb up, knuckles forward, and your right hand is open, also thumb up, knuckles forward. The pinkie of the right hand is a few inches away from the point where the leash is connected to the collar. This is the "reining position" (figure 7). If you tell your dog to sit now and he

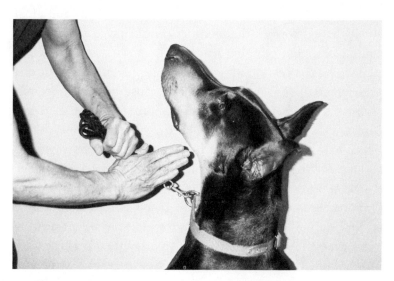

Figure 7. Reining position.

doesn't, rein the leash up and toward you with your right hand, in the same direction and with the same force you applied to the collar. Be careful not to tug or jerk the leash. You want just enough steady pressure to help the dog choose the correct response.

- Continue anywhere from five to fifteen minutes (with a few breaks for playtime). Be sure to quit with your dog still eager for more! Don't wait for him to become bored or tired.
- Don't forget to master this command while you're in the full, upright, and locked position—standing tall. Go back to page 74 if you need help remembering the sit-kneel-stand progression.

As with the Food/Toy/Play Method, do a few sessions in the same location before moving to another room and eventually to the great outdoors.

GETTING OFF THE CHUCK WAGON
(What your dog doesn't want you to know)

Those of you using the Food/Toy Method, pay close attention! Those who've used the Touchy-Feely Method can either skip ahead to "Correcting the Sit" (page 80) or read this and gloat about the extra work the food/toy people have to do! Or you could go ice your pitching arm again.

After a few sessions, it will become apparent that your dog understands "sit." You will know because he will automatically sit whenever he sees the food lure. Or because he sits constantly, all day long, in hopes of getting a reward. Or because he used to weigh fifteen pounds and now weighs eighty! Any of these developments indicate that you've done a great job teaching the "sit" command. Now we move on to "random reinforcement." That's a fancy phrase that simply means you will give your dog the reward *randomly* instead of *every* time she does the sit. I like to call this the Three-Card Monte approach. There used to be guys on the streets of

New York City (maybe there still are) who pulled this con, a card game they let you win a few times, until you liked it, and then they'd have you. Winning is addictive for dogs, too! When I initiate random reinforcement, I give the reward for the first sit, then the third and fifth, and so on. Next time, I'll give it for the first, the fifth, and the twelfth. "Random" means just that, so don't fall into a predictable pattern. Low-confidence dogs may need a longer time to be weaned off the treats, while dogs with a really high food/play drive can wean very quickly—they maintain their enthusiasm no matter how infrequent the reward. Your objective is to get your dog to per-form without *any* food or toy. That's not to say that there won't be anything in it for him. It's more of a "switcheroo." Every time you release him with "Okay" you give him a verbal reward—"Good job! Aren't you smart!"—petting him and making him feel like the best dog in the world. You just aren't handing out the food. Can you guess what your dog's response will be? (Not the initial response: "Hmm, maybe she forgot my cookie. Hey, lemme do that sit for you again. Wait a minute, what's up with this?") No, I mean the mother of all responses, the canine "Talk to the hand" response, the "What have you done for me *lately*?" response. Ah, yes, the dreaded, stone-cold . . .

NO COOKIE, NO SITTY

You know of this response? Ah, perhaps you have a teenager in your house, too! Or a two-year-old. In any event, this is the time that a *negative correction* needs to be applied. "Negative correction" sounds so, well, *negative*. Think of it as tough love. You see, you don't *want* your dog's obedience dependent on food or toys. Either was just a temporary bribe, scheduled to run out as soon as he got the message. You may not have his special spider or a nickel-sized slice of cheese stick at hand when he runs out the front door at five a.m. And you probably can't keep liver in your pajamas. Further-more, he may not be in a particularly hungry or playful mood. Any of these possibilities do not change the fact that he MUST obey a command he has been taught. He has his unruly impulses, but a truly trained dog must show impulse control. *Why,* you may ask, would an animal override his impulses, to run, bark, poop, or whatever they may be? Simply put, BECAUSE YOU SAID SO, assuming of course that your relationship with the dog is based on a solid foundation of training, play, and love. But whether or not they feel all these things in equal measure all the time, my dogs never lose sight of a simple reality: If I say it, they will do it. That's the power of training, of course, not nature. How do we achieve this kind of compliance?

First, I have to define a correction. A correction is something done to a dog who *understands* the command but is *choosing* not to obey. He might be distracted. It could be he thinks he *has* a choice. In any case, while never abusive, a correction is something your dog always wants to avoid. For some dogs a quiet "ah-ah" said without harshness is sufficient. For others it may be a gentle tug on the leash. Others will need something in between. Remember, the goal is to *instruct,* not to *punish,* the latter implying a level of suffering. The distinction is all-important. You simply want your dog to understand that his response to the command is incorrect.

It is a waste of time to apply correction to a dog who doesn't understand the command (go back and retrain), or a dog who has been spooked by a loud noise and out of fear wouldn't sit (go back and retrain with distractions—we are coming to this).

CORRECTING THE SIT

In this section you will learn how to correct a dog who isn't sitting or is sitting too slowly. While you are reading this, remember *who* you have at the end of the leash in deciding which correction will work best.

A "pop" is a gentle tug on the leash, ranging from mild to sharp. You want to use the least amount of force necessary to make your point. First, for an effective pop, the leash will need to be a bit slack before you tug (a taut leash produces a different sensation when tugged, more of a dragging feeling—think tug-of-war—which is ineffective as a correction). My advice to students is to hook the leash to something sturdy (the arm of a large chair, a fence, your spouse—just kidding!) and practice popping before applying the move to the dog. Practice makes perfect, and the more decisive your pop, the more effective it will be.

Second, please remember that a correction is always applied *without emotion*. Don't pop in anger. Your dog can tell. You're simply pointing out faulty behavior, and you should betray no more passion than an electric fence. After a correction, you will need to double your normal praise when the dog obeys.

Let's run through the mechanics of a correction in the context of a sit.

- Holding the leash (attached to your dog, whom you've trained to sit), say your dog's name and "sit."
- If your dog sits, praise ("Good boy") and when ready, release ("Okay").
- Your dog starts to sit, but then notices your neighbor's new puppy and stands up.
- You give a mild pop on the leash without repeating the command. Your dog looks back at you and sits.
- Say, "Yes!" then praise (Good sit") and release ("Okay").
- A mild pop gets you a burp instead of the required sit. He is now staring at you. . . .
- Give a slightly harder pop on the leash, still without repeating the command.
- If the dog sits, say, "Yes!" then praise ("Good sit") and release ("Okay").
- If you still don't get a sit, pop a bit harder. If that's not effective, put your hands on his collar (steering position) and pressure up and in until he sits.
- Say, "Yes!" then praise ("Good sit") and release ("Okay").

If you popped your dog three times and there was no response from him, you have to stop and re-evaluate. Ask yourself if you've taught the behavior as thoroughly as possible. Perhaps there is some confusion (in your dog's mind) as to what "sit" really means. If there is even a *remote* chance that the dog is confused, go back and retrain for a few days. It's not the end of the world! Good training often depends on taking one step backward to take two more forward. When it comes to corrections, I would rather err on the side of caution. It's better to mistakenly retrain a dog who is feeling willful than to correct a dog who is simply confused. Correcting a confused dog is not merely uninstructive, but leads to stress, fear, and damage to the positive training relationship you are creating. When in doubt, retrain!

For the Hydraulic Sitters in Your Life . . .

Every now and again there will be a dog who immediately takes to sitting on command, but does so slowly. Very slowly. You could have a grande latte in the time it takes him to sit! Such sluggishness could signify a confidence problem or a power struggle, or a slow sit could just be his style. If lack of confidence is to blame for his slowness, with a little more time he should speed up on his own. If he doesn't, then we are dealing with one of the other two issues, both of which can be effectively answered in the same way.

The key is to speed up the sit without causing the dog to think he is being corrected for sitting. A bit tricky, but try this and he should soon be going with the flow.

- Play "I've Got Your Butt"
  When your hydraulic sitter begins his majestic descent, reach out quickly and push his butt into a sit. Release with "okay." Repeat. Be mindful of how you do this. You are *not* slam-dunking your dog; you are giving him a gentle but decisive push into the sit. If he comes to see it as a game, soon he will be trying to beat you by sitting before you can "get his butt."

- Correction

    You start out just as in "Correcting the Sit" (page 80), but when you make the correction on a slow sitter, *do* repeat the word "sit" as you apply a gentle tug on the leash. I know: after all I've said about not repeating, blah blah blah. That's why correcting the slow sitter is tricky. Understand that if the dog in any way perceives this correction to mean he shouldn't be sitting, you are sunk! Repeating "sit" while tugging his collar is meant to reinforce the message that he was doing the right thing, just not fast enough for your liking. As soon as you see an increase in speed, drop the extra command and praise profusely!

    Continue working on the sit a few more times until your dog starts to show the first signs of fatigue or boredom. (Always leave 'em wanting more!) After a few successful sits, end the session with what is appropriate for your type of dog. Are you drawing a blank? Come on, I know you remember this part! Okay, let's review: Low-energy or low-confidence dog? End the session with a fun game or a special treat. However, try the same treatment with a dominant, power-struggling dog and you'll end up flushing the whole session down the, er, powder room. That type of dog is better served if you crate or confine him for fifteen to twenty minutes after the session. Confinement impresses on him how much fun you and your training sessions are (as opposed to how boring his comfy crate can be). Seems unfair? We're after results, not justice. Besides, the crate is not unpleasant; it's simply not stimulating. (Your dog is already overstimulated.) Pop quiz: If you let him jump on your couch immediately after training, how do you suppose he would rate the lesson experience vs. the couch experience? Draw your own conclusions—he certainly will. Follow this counsel, and as your training progresses and you and your dog become more of a team, you may notice that the once dominant and training-averse dog has become more excited by your sessions. That's what we're after. You can then reduce or eliminate the post-training isolation. Like a teenager, your dog will constantly be evolving during the training process. It's your job to keep track of who he is and what his needs are from day to day.

Final and very important note: If your dog exhibits any aggression at your corrections, be it growling, biting, or anything in between, you need the help of a professional at your side throughout the training process. Such behavior is *not* caused by a pop on the leash. It's a sign of issues that need to be addressed professionally, and if they aren't, the behavior will continue with growing frequency and intensity. Inquire at a local dog club for names of private trainers. A professional can diagnose the problem and perhaps give you a quick and effective solution so that you can go back to training your dog on your own again. Aggression is not something a layperson should diagnose *or* treat.

A DISTRACTING SITUATION
(The forced error)

If you're like most of my clients, you would no more consider inducing an obedience blunder in your dog than you would hiring someone to mow the lawn around the building where your kid is taking the SAT. But unlike the Big Test, obedience training is not simply a hurdle your dog has to clear once. If he doesn't get used to compliance in unpredictable, high-pressure situations, his judgment might fail him when it matters most (in automobile traffic, for instance).

When you purposefully cause a dog to screw up because of distraction (also called *proofing*), you are teaching him *under what circumstances you expect him to obey.* (By now, you should know that would be *all* circumstances.) For example, say your dog is a genius about sitting. When you are alone with him. In

your living room. You both feel pretty good about his profi-
ciency—until you go outside and he sees a bird. You say, "Sit";
and he says, "See ya!" If you're lucky, you had the leash on him
and were able to correct him for not sitting. You may think you
have just discovered the limits of his sitting genius. But really
you have just exposed the limits of what he's been taught. His
mental file on the word "sit" is not very big—yet. It contains
only the instructions he has learned so far about sitting—
something to be done in your quiet living room. The next step
is to fill out his command file to the point where he reliably
performs what's asked, no matter what is going on around
him. And here's some uplifting news: With each subsequent
command you teach, this broadening phase will require less
work. Once the dog understands how to work through distractions, he will learn to factor them out more quickly when
learning any new behavior.

The Loss of Innocence

I know, you don't want "Sweetums" to think you are some
trickster leading him down the road to perdition when all he
wants is to please you. Don't worry, he won't. He'll just learn
that your commands take precedence over his drives and
desires. The right decision could save his life! When you teach
the "come" command so well that your dog will come even as
a cat races ahead of him into the road, you won't regret this
minor underhandedness, believe me. But for now, let's work
on distractions as they pertain to "sit."

Distractions should be very slight at the start and gradually increase in degree of challenge. As with motivators, the
nature of distractions depends on the individual. What is difficult (perhaps inconceivable) for a food-driven dog to ignore
(a dog cookie at his feet, for instance) might pose no challenge
for a dog that is into toys. It should go without saying that the
dog should *never* be purposefully distracted by anything
potentially harmful. You may trick him for his own good, but
letting anything bad happen to him is not only unethical but
destructive to your relationship, which must be built on trust.

Allowing kids to ride bikes or throw baseballs too close to the dog is too risky to be justified in the name of instruction.

The Three Distraction Factors

- External stimulus: The doorbell ringing, kids running around, surprise appearance of a motivator (a piece of food dropping to the floor), a chipmunk running in your yard, etc.
- Range: How far you are from the dog. He's used to training up close and personal, but he needs to be reliable up to fifty yards (or more!) away.
- Duration: How long he can obey on his own before succumbing to distraction. Initially you clock duration in seconds; later on, in minutes; eventually building up to twenty minutes (if you need his duration time to be longer, then you should really consider using a crate or otherwise confining your dog).

In the early training stages, you can build distraction resistance one factor at a time, but as your dog gets better at ignoring temptation, he will become ready for multivariable distractions, provided you take care to increase the number and intensity of the various factors gradually. The more thoroughly you have typed your dog, the more efficiently you can zero in on and reduce his susceptibility to his individual distractions.

Here's an example of training with distractions:

Dog type: mildly food motivated; average to high toy drive
External stimulus: flying tennis ball
Distraction theater: kitchen area (close-quarters distraction)

- Owner holds subject Spicy by the leash. Owner throws the tennis ball, and, as Spicy follows trajectory, owner commands, "Spicy, sit."

- Spicy seems to be using an alias or ignoring the "sit" command. She is off to investigate the tennis ball. Is Spicy bad? No! Stupid? Hardly! Spiteful? Get over yourself! Spicy is just WRONG! This is no occasion for anger and recriminations. Just gentle correction. Remember, we are not after a pound of flesh, but an ounce of prevention.
- Spicy's owner *calmly* (no anger) walks over, *gently* takes her by the collar (no anger), leading her back to scene of the "sit" command she ignored and firmly but not roughly (no anger) physically enforces a sit. The usual "Yes!" praise, and release with "Okay" follow the correction.
- Owner repeats the same distraction with the ball, and guess what. Spicy goes off to investigate again! This time the owner, better prepared, has a firm grip on the leash and doesn't give Spicy enough slack to flee the sit spot despite her obvious intent to do so. Since the first correction wasn't effective, the owner gives a mild pop on the leash. This gets Spicy's attention, and she promptly sits. "Yes!" praise, and release with "Okay" follow.

If Spicy had not responded to the pop, a gradual escalation of the corrections would have been indicated. First, however, a question. Is your chosen distraction simply too stimulating for the dog? Sometimes it will be, and the difficulty in resisting a distraction depends not on the nature of the stimulus (remember "What dog could resist STEAK?"), but rather on the nature of the dog. Know thy dog. In the case of a suspected superstimulus you would be better served to back up and proceed more slowly. For instance, if Spicy *hadn't* responded to leash pops and her owner got the sense that the tennis ball was making her wild, the owner could have started by rolling the ball instead of throwing it. This would make the exercise easier for the dog to handle. One can always build back up gradually to the original degree of difficulty.

Note on distractors: You might discover in a superstimulating distraction something better used as a motivator. If that tennis ball proves beguiling, and you don't live near the U.S. Open, where such a distraction is likely to appear with regularity, ask whether it might not benefit you to use the ball as a motivator. This does not mean it's not still a distraction factor we must train for, only that it has a dual use. Although SnookyBaBa can learn to fetch the paper and even bring you just the sports section for a piece of hot dog, his enthusiasm for this reward must be in control. Say you were having a barbecue and Aunt Bertha was using her hotdog in a bun to illustrate how tiny her peony plants were at the beginning of the season. SnookyBaBa must be taught not to attempt the old "drive-by" hit to snag Auntie's tempting weiner. Impulse control is what we're after here. Good for everyone in the long run, most immediately Aunt Bertha.

Fortunately, Spicy has mastered the tennis-ball distraction. Her owner now needs to test her in different locations to be sure she understands that "sit" means sit *wherever* a tennis ball may appear. Not just in the kitchen, not just in the house, not just in the yard, but *anywhere*. After that, the owner will move on to other distractions and more locations until Spicy has seen it all and will, come what may, sit on command!

In the Rain, on a Train, in a House, with a Mouse

The following are some distraction factors to be tried first with the "sit" command. Start with these and add your own as you discover things most likely to lead *your* dog to stray. Remember, distractions to some degree should reflect your lifestyle—if you live on a dairy farm, doing a sit near the fence of the cow pasture might be useful, but city dwellers might want to perfect the sit in the presence of buses and trucks before tackling anything with a cloven hoof.

- Location, location, location: upstairs, downstairs, inside, outside
- Common neighborhood stimuli: strangers in the night, a neighbor's barbecue, kids on bikes, a "flying saucer," or at least a Frisbee
- All-terrain canine: changing the sit surface—grass, tile, pavement, gravel, *wet* grass! (He won't, without practice, be equally delighted to plant himself on all of these.)
- Temptation afoot: having a toy or a piece of food on the ground
- Backseat driver: holding the sit while a second person is talking to him—build up to the other person petting him
- Animals on parade: other dogs (on leash!) in the same room or area

Once these distractions are attempted individually, you should experiment with multivariable distractions, working sit amid combinations of external variables: kids riding past on bikes, car-horn blasts (check local noise-pollution fines before trying that one), airplane flyovers, hot-dog vendors opening for business.

How much distraction should the dog learn to bear? As much as he's likely to encounter in the sort of world you inhabit, and then some. While he doesn't need to be ready for combat, like a good soldier he should be equal to the toughest conditions he might encounter. Provide him a margin of error.

Proceed at the pace *your* dog can handle and build up—individuals vary as to strengths and weakenesses. If your dog is easily distracted, patience will be rewarded. One fine day, you will throw that ball as you give the "sit" command, and he will look at you impassively as if to say, "Nice try!"

Look, Ma, No Leash!

Once you have a proofed sit command on a leash, you'll want to teach your dog to do it off leash. Why? Because a sit without a wait is nice, but for practical purposes it's only a little more useful than rolling over. If your dog breaks the sit to bound forward when you've dropped the pot roast or your guests come through the door, that sit could fast become a joke.

Put your dog on either a fifteen- or twenty-foot leash or on your flexi locked out to the full twenty-six feet. The leash will be on the floor during the entire training session and you have to pinkie-swear that you won't touch it. Next, make sure you're in a quiet, confined area and that your dog is hungry, lonely, and/or bored.

Now we can begin: Tell your dog to sit. If he does, you know the drill—praise, reward (randomly at first, then fading the reward away), and release.

If he doesn't wait, choosing instead to walk away or toward you or to leave the room, start walking down the leash (remember the tightrope?) until you arrive at your not-yet-sitting dog. Slowly reach for his collar with one hand, take him back to the spot he was in when you gave him the command, and give it a tug. This correction mimics the pop you would be giving if you were holding the leash. When he sits, praise, reward, release. Those of you whose dogs didn't move and just stood there (or maybe went down), walk to your dog, reach slowly for his collar and give it a tug.

The initial, and perhaps even subsequent noncompliance was likely the result of your dog not feeling the usual leash tension on his collar. That caused him to hypothesize that sitting was optional, and he tested that theory. You're probably thinking, "Why, after all the work I did in teaching and distracting the sit would he ever imagine such a thing?" Maybe your language was a little saltier. The reason could be that before you started formally training him, you were in the habit of calling out commands that he either didn't understand or that you failed to enforce. You fixed that problem on leash, but now that we're in the virtual off-leash mode, he's having flash-backs. Or, there is the less psychoanalytic reason: YOU NEVER TAUGHT HIM HE HAD TO DO THIS OFF LEASH. Don't depend on a dog to draw inferences; every deviation is a different ball game to him. Off leash is just another distraction for which the sit must be proofed.

For dogs who are baffled by the concept of doing a sit anywhere but at your feet, you may tie the leash to something stationary (use your judgment: for toy dogs it might be a doorknob, for large dogs try the leg of a large sturdy table). With the dog thus anchored, stand a few feet away and tell him to sit. If you've done a good job estimating his strength, your dog will either be sitting pretty or vainly struggling to move forward. Now you walk in, gently correct the dog for not sitting, then praise, release, and reward. Gradually increase the distance and change the location before attempting this without a tether.

Once your dog will do an immediate sit without need of a correction, in whatever spot you told him to do it, then you're free to move ahead. When you've proofed the remote-control sit (with appropriate distractions), you're ready to return to your original quiet area and start working him without the leash, free as he was born.

But what can you do to correct a sit when the leash is gone and you're several feet away? You still have your hands, and he's still wearing his collar. If he decides not to sit, calmly and slowly walk toward him, avoiding eye contact, with your arm outstretched. This may take a minute, it may take twenty, however, regardless of the duration of your walk-down, when you finally reach him, your correction will be the same. Gently take him by the collar, calmly leading him back to the spot where he was when you gave the command and tug up on his collar to correct him. Praise, reward, and release. If you started walking him down at 8 a.m. and finally got to him at lunchtime, this is an indication that you probably didn't meet the criteria for a perfect sit on a drag leash. Or your idea of a "confined area" was too broad-ranging. No harm, no foul—go back and make sure he is 100 percent perfect on leash. The beautiful part of my training program is the self-imposed honor system: Cheat a little now, and you'll be redoing it later.

WARNING: As you have not yet taught him to come when called, you should be working him only in confined areas—a fenced yard, rooms in the house, a squash court, etc.

DURATION: TEACHING "WAIT"

The definition of a perfect sit-wait: The handler (speaking in a moderate but firm tone of voice) says, "Sit," and then, "Wait." The dog holds the sit as the handler walks away. The dog's feet never move. And although the dog may look around, nothing that catches his attention makes him break the sit. There is no sniffing at the ground, no scratching his ears, and certainly no personal-hygiene gestures (especially common in male dogs). It is as if his feet were cast in cement. The dog remains motionless until the handler returns to his side and then releases him with the signal "Okay."

That's the textbook scenario. Here's the Hollywood version of that same sit-wait: *A majestic dog sits high upon a mountain-top, the cool breeze rustling his glossy fur. But wait—what's that sound? A rabbit leaps from the brush charging straight toward the noble canine (hey, anything is possible with special effects). Every fiber of the dog's being quivers, his deepest instincts commanding him to give chase, but . . . he does not succumb. His soulful eyes come to rest on the solitary figure twenty-five yards away. That man told him to sit and stay three hours ago. That man, even if he has forgotten his own command (as the dog is beginning to suspect) nevertheless enjoys the dog's unconditional love. The distant sight of the man this dog knows simply as Pa, and the (even more distant) memory of his inviolable command makes the dog sit a little taller, a little straighter, proud to be an American dog. Roll credits.*

Makes *me* proud to own a dog (sniff)! But before you need

your own hankie, you'll need to do some work. With smart training, even your dog could do his own stunts in the Hollywood version.

The Checklist

Almost the same list as for "Teaching 'Sit.' " I'll give you the abbreviated version here; go back and reread the "Teaching 'Sit' " section (page 68) if this doesn't jog your memory.

1. Ready dog: hungry, lonely, and/or bored
2. Ready known motivator
3. Be sure your dog is wearing a collar and a four- to six-foot leash. As you increase your distance you may switch to a longer leash or a flexi.
4. Go to a quiet, distraction-free area.
5. The "wait" command will be taught with you standing up.
6. Your dog must demonstrate *thorough* understanding of the command that precedes the "wait," which in this case is the "sit." (The same procedure for teaching "sit and wait" applies to teaching "down and wait," but the sit is an easier position in which to introduce the wait, since the former is the dog's first, and therefore most ingrained, command.)

Here we go.

*   Pick a spot on the floor, which you'll mark with a small piece of electrical tape, masking tape, a chalk line, or one of your kid's Barney stickers—just make sure you and the dog can see it. This will be his mark, and if he breaks the sit, you'll return him to the exact spot. If you don't reset him in the exact spot (and that alternative spot just happens to be closer to you), he will learn to gain ground by breaking his wait.
*   Start with your dog standing over his mark, on your left, his attached leash in your right hand.

- Your motivator (food or toy) is hidden in your right hand.
- Tell your dog to sit.
- When the dog sits, say, "Yes!" followed by the word . . .
- . . . "wait," which is given simultaneously with the following signal: your left hand, fingers together, palm down a few inches above the dog's eyes (figure 8).

Figure 8. "Wait" hand signal.

Figure 9. Pivot in front of dog.

- Discontinue the signal immediately (let your hand drop back down to your side).
- Pivot in front of the dog so that you are *no more than twelve inches* away from him (figure 9).
- Count five seconds (one–one thousand, two–one thousand, etc.).
- If your dog has stayed perfectly still, check his pulse. (Sorry, I couldn't resist! Almost no dog does this right the first time.)
- If your dog has stayed perfectly still for the five seconds, pivot back to his right side so that the two of you are facing the same direction (figure 10).
- Praise ("Good boy"; "Good dog"), reward, and release ("Okay").

This Dog Can't Wait

If your dog did stay, congratulations! Go do a 5K while the rest of us keep working, and meet us back at the "Distractions on the Side" section (page 98). Most dogs won't be mesmerized by the palm of your hand for long, however deep your love line may be. Your dog will have more likely broken the sit be-

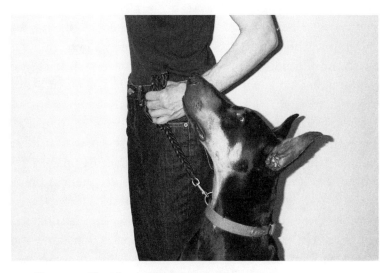

Figure 10. Pivot back to dog's right side.

fore you could praise. How's he supposed to know what that hand meant?

Help him along by decreasing the time you expect him to stay (try a three-second stay instead of a fiver). He may have misunderstood your pivoting in front of him. Try remaining next to him until he's figured out that you want him to hold the sit. If at any point he tries to get up, gently re-sit him (simultaneously saying, "sit") in the exact spot he started in, and repeat the command "wait." Yes, you heard me, *repeat* the command. When you repeat a command while physically re-inforcing the command, that's called training. Repeating a command endlessly while doing nothing is called blathering! At the first sign of waiting, give lots of praise and encourage-ment. If he's still finding the command hard to grasp, try mov-ing to a quieter environment. (Closets don't count!)

Is my dog so nervous or insecure that he is breaking his stay just to be close to me?

Only you can judge. Some dogs are so anxiously clingy, especially when beginning to train, that they will break a stay just for the sake of being near their owners, even knowing that it's the wrong move (and that they will be corrected). My golden retriever Opal had this problem when first learning to wait. Initially the remedy for it is to "re-place" the dog (I mean gently return her to her place, not get a new dog), reducing the duration of the stay and the distance you move away. In other words, make the lesson to be learned "smaller," just as you would do for a dog who was confused by the command. After a while, though, I felt that Opal wasn't disobeying in good faith. She was *choosing* fearfulness over progress, in spite of all my reassuring efforts. She'd seen enough to know that there was no danger in learning to wait, but she decided just to dig in her heels (figuratively), or rather not to dig them in (more literally). I therefore introduced a mild correction (in her case a pop on the leash), levying a tax, so to speak, on her undesir-able choice of noncooperation ("Vee have vays of making you vait"). She quickly realized that, while being near me was heaven, it wasn't worth getting corrected for it! In addition, I made the release so much fun that she focused on getting to that reward rather than getting to me.

I don't give a woof.

Got a shameless scofflaw on that leash? After a week of teaching "wait," you can move to the correction stage. Here's how to correct a dog who won't hold his sit:

1. At the first sign of movement, step into the dog's "personal" space, and, still facing him, pop lightly up on the leash. In the case of a dog who learned the sit via the physical method, you should pop up on the collar while simultaneously tucking his back end into a sit with your hand. That should re-sit him in the same spot. If he has gone too far from his mark, bring him all the way back to his mark, pop lightly, and *only then* repeat the "sit" command.

2. Tell him to wait, and take a step back. If he doesn't hold the sit, keep repeating step 1 until he does. Keep in mind that if your dog's reason for breaking his wait is that he's distracted or feels he has a choice, the force of your pop may have to be increased. Confused or fearful dogs need shorter distances and shorter time frames.

3. When he successfully holds the sit for five seconds, draw near again, facing him. Pivot back to the start position so that he is on your left and you are facing the same direction.

4. Praise, reward, and release.

Important detail: If, as you approach your dog, he breaks his sit before you can release him by saying, "Okay," *put him back!* He doesn't understand that you were about to release him and shouldn't be anticipating your actions anyway. The break must be treated like any other display of wrongheaded willfulness, plain and simple. After you re-place him, leave again and work on his response to your return.

If the popping and pressing don't work, you may need to

reconsider the training collar. A physically tough dog may be more readily convinced to wait (or sit or down, etc.) in a collar that distributes the tug differently. See chapter 3 for the equipment options. Or, maybe your dog isn't hungry, lonely, and/or bored. Maybe he's full, sick of you, and over-stimulated. You can't outsmart the checklist. Always make sure you've stacked all the biscuits in your favor before you start training!

When your dog has completed three five-second sit-waits, you may increase the wait time to ten seconds, and then fifteen. The first goal is to have your dog do a sit-wait for one minute with you twelve inches away from him.

After that, drop the time back down to five seconds, and add two feet to your distance. This is also the point that you start rewarding your dog randomly. Now, now, don't fret. Review the concept by going back to page 78, and remember that although the food and toys will ultimately be gone, your praise and love will always be a major part of training. Once you can get fifteen feet away from your dog for five seconds, increase the time to ten seconds. If you have a full one-minute sit-wait at fifteen feet, congratulations! Move on to the distractions section below. Yes, you have to. No, don't close the book. Hey, get back here! Sit!

DISTRACTIONS ON THE SIDE

After your dog has achieved the goal of a one-minute sit-wait, you need to start introducing distractions. In my method, distractions are to training what coleslaw is to a cheeseburger in a diner: You may not have ordered it, but you should always expect it to be served on the side. It's crucial that your dog's understanding be deeper than the puddle of a best-case scenario. Life is messy; his sense of duty must transcend that mess. When you add distractions to his sit-wait, remain very near him at first so that you can get to him quickly when he breaks the sit. Now, as to the nature of distractions, a very wise dog trainer once said, "Distractions should be very slight at the start and gradually increase in degree of challenge. As with motivators, the nature of distractions depends on the individual. What is difficult (perhaps inconceivable) for a food-driven dog to ignore (a dog cookie at his feet, for instance) might pose no challenge for a dog that is into toys. It should go without saying that the dog must *never* be purposefully distracted by anything potentially harmful." Gosh, that sounds *so* familiar. . . .

When your dog defies a distraction's challenge to his concentration, he is obeying to the nth degree—i.e., not merely doing what you *just* said, but remembering, and remembering, and doing it until your release. What a guy! Watch him ignore that dog cookie, but don't underestimate the effort required. That stillness, which may appear to be nothing, is a big something (think of those guards at Buckingham Palace!), and it needs proper recognition. *While* your dog is performing this feat—not moving even when presented with the most powerful temptation—you need to be praising him. As usual, quiet praise will do for the high-drive dog, more exuberant praise for the low-confidence dog. You don't have to be next to your dog to praise him. In fact, if he breaks the "sit-wait" *because* you praised him, you may go in and correct him—provided you are sure he knows the difference between the praise words and the release ("Okay"). If he doesn't know the difference, you may need to do some remedial work on the release concept. Make sure you always use the same word—"Okay"—and use it only to mean "You're done!"

Anyway, back to specific distractions to challenge your dog's waiting skills. A list of my favorites follows, but feel free to create your own, based on your dog's type. Remember to correct any unauthorized movement (apart from looking side to side), no matter how small!

- *A little tension on the leash.* This simple trick will make the dog work harder to hold the sit during the "wait" command. (The natural impulse is to yield.) It is the equivalent of a runner training while wearing ankle weights.

- *Clap your hands.* There's an unwritten rule in the dog code that if someone is clapping it means run over to that person. You have to teach your dog that this isn't so.
- *Speaking in tongues.* Prattle to your dog in a high-pitched squeaky voice as if you've lost all worldly sense. "Ohhh, what a cutie pie!"; "I just *love* puppy-wuppy dogs," etc. This is of *huge* benefit in teaching your dog to ignore the kind of tones he will hear from many strangers. It usually stimulates the dog to the point of jumping on the squawker—ironic, because people who most dislike being jumped on are the ones most prone to address the dog this way. Even more ironic, shrieking, "Don't jump on me!" always has the opposite effect from the one intended. Once your dog can tolerate *your* speaking in tongues, have your friends and neighbors do the same thing. Before that, make sure any new speaker starts out talking quietly to the dog, for example, a soft "Hi, puppy."
- *Location changes.* Each and every room in your house. Your yard. Sidewalks. Ball fields. Playgrounds. As your dog's confidence and skill increase, so should the difficulty of the distraction. Macy's Thanksgiving parade anyone?
- *Eliminating the food or toy reward.* You've been giving it randomly, now move to "once in a blue moon." To certain dogs this is the most distracting situation of all.
- *Disappearing Act.* Your dog has to learn to wait even if you're not in the room. Begin by standing directly behind him—a few feet at first, then build up to a longer distance. Correct any movement other than the swiveling of his head. When he's comfortable with you behind him, progress to walking out of—and then directly back into—the room. Gradually increase the length of time you're gone as he increases his ability to stay when you're not eyeballing him into position. You must always be able to see your dog in the teaching phase, so keep checking over your shoulder when you're walking away. Don't

forget to peek around the corner while you're in the next room to monitor his progress. Otherwise, you may think he's sitting and waiting, but what he's actually done is plopped himself down on the couch and is going to town on that new beaded pillow you just bought. Save the pillow; watch the dog.

See "A Distracting Situation" on page 84 for more ideas.

This above all: Be patient! "Wait" is a difficult concept to grasp and execute. Mastery will take more than a few days of work. There are many common forms of distraction, but each must be programmed separately. Your dog's knowing that "wait" means he can't chase a ball does *not* mean he won't chase a kid with a hot dog. Expecting him to make that kind of complex generalization is wishful thinking—for now, anyway. In fact, the more your dog learns, the better a thinker he will become.

Reality Check from the Major Leagues
(Or, "The Stepford Dogs")

A dog that competes in AKC Obedience trials is expected to hold a sit-wait for one minute and a down-stay for three minutes. This, while standing in a line of a dozen other dogs he has never seen before, dogs of every size, shape, and breed. These strangers are not only off leash and a mere arm's length away; they are also twenty-five feet away from their owners across the ring. Let me not mention the dogs barking, jumping, and carrying on with other exercises in the next ring. Or the ring-side food stands, whose offerings include . . . HOT DOGS! Did I mention that these requirements pertain to the Novice level?

In the more advanced Open class, the minimum duration of a sit is three minutes and the shortest for a down-wait is five; the handlers are totally out of sight, having left the ring. But guess what? Thanks to months of training, the dogs handle the tests just fine. They do well *not* because they have "professional" trainers, although of course some of them do. And *not* because they are selected from special blood lines genetically modified for extreme obedience, although some degree of aptitude can be bred for, just as a certain kind of coloring can. For all intents and purposes, these dogs, whatever their native gifts or circumstantial advantages, started out knowing absolutely nothing. Just like your dog. How did they turn into such models of decorum, appearing to be virtual "Stepford Dogs"? There's nothing mysterious or sinister about it: They followed a good training plan and were the beneficiaries of lavish patience. It's a pretty safe bet that none of those dogs, who seem always to know what is expected, trained solely in their owners' living rooms or quiet backyards. They were trained with distractions in different locations until they achieved 100 percent understanding. That, by the way, is your goal whether or not you dream of your dog being High in Trial. (Breed dogs win Best in Show; obedience dogs win High in Trial.)

Nothing worth doing is ever easy. Ribbons are nice, but a dog's waiting on a mountaintop as bunnies frolic around him is its own reward.

TEACHING "DOWN"

Definition of a perfect down: The handler (in a calm but firm tone of voice) says, "[Dog's name], down." No matter what is happening around him, or anything else he might be doing, the dog immediately assumes a prone position, the handler never repeating the command, snapping his fingers, raising his voice, bending at the waist, or otherwise contorting himself.

Sounds familiar? It should, since it's practically the same as the definition of the perfect sit. Actually it's simplified for rhetorical effect: You are going to teach your dog to lie down in two different positions—in front of you and beside you. Oh, how *fan-cy*!

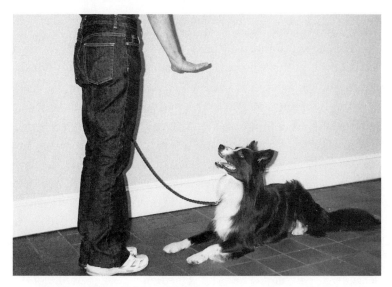

Figure 11. "Down" from in front.

The Frontal Approach

Your dog lies down as you face each other (figure 11). The most common use of this down is to stop or prevent his forward movement. Perhaps you have just called him, but, as he approaches, you see your two-year-old niece, who is deathly afraid of dogs, coming out of the kitchen. Being able to stop your dog by making him lie down instantly neutralizes a potentially bad situation. (The prone position is even more reassuring than a sit, which he can break faster.) Or, maybe you broke a glass in the kitchen, and as you were starting to clean it up you notice your dog coming around the corner to investigate. Here again, having the instant down is like an emergency brake that can save you an emergency visit to the vet!

We will use a hand signal along with a verbal command in the teaching stages, but as your dog progresses you'll have the option of using *either* alone. By the way, a hand signal that tells your dog to lie down is especially impressive when you have company.

The other down you will be teaching is the . . .

Curled Down

This down (figure 12) starts with your dog sitting at your left side in heel position. The American Kennel Club Obedience regulations defines the heel position as: *Whether the dog is sitting, standing, lying down or moving, the dog shall be in line with the direction the handler is facing, at the handler's left side, and as close to the handler's left side as practical, permitting the handler freedom of motion at all times. The area from the dog's head to shoulder shall be in line with the handler's left hip.* "Oh, no! Long sentences printed in italics! What was that again?" Now aren't you glad that this book is not written like the instruction manual of your DVD player? You can thank me later. Meanwhile, do NOT skip ahead to the "Teaching 'Here' " section (page 136)! The AKC Obedience Police will *not* be knocking on your door checking for correct heel compliance. That's just a guideline! But you do need to make sure your dog is on your left side, fairly close to you, and facing the same direction. Simple enough? Okay. When told to "curl," your dog will lie down and roll onto his left hip.

You'll use the curled down when you want your dog to stay down for extended periods of time, up to fifteen minutes. Your dog *can* learn to stay for much longer but I find that, gen-

Figure 12. Curled down at side.

erally, after fifteen minutes he is no longer comfortable and you are no longer paying close attention. The latter undermines the training: If he moves, you must correct him, but you won't be able to if you're not paying strict attention. And if you fail to correct even after a long wait, you are sending a mixed message about the command: "Sometimes you *can* break the down-wait and get away with it." Such equivocation in training is not fair to the dog. If you need to park him for more than fifteen minutes, your dog would be much happier confined somewhere with a nice toy. That way, you can keep your mind on what you're doing and he can entertain himself.

Danger, Will Robinson!
Read This *Before* You Get Started!

Teaching the down is another huge milestone in your dog's training career. The sit taught him to learn, and the wait taught him the range of circumstances under which he was to obey. The down, as your dog's ultimate submission, will reiterate or perhaps *define* who is the leader in your pack. (Dogs don't believe everyone's created equal—there was never a canine Enlightenment!) Because "down" teaches that you're the boss, dominance issues, not manifested while teaching "sit," can make their first appearance when teaching and enforcing the "down" command. I've seen responses in a wide range of forms: in a minor vein, a dog grumbling a little on his way down. After a swift correction, this one will change his tune fast: "Whoa, hey, no one ever explained to me that *you're* the boss around here! Here's that down you wanted. Anything else I can do for you, chief?" Of course, there is also the other end of the spectrum. After being gently guided into a down for the first time, another dog may launch himself teeth first at the handler, trainer, or whoever was unfortunate enough to be holding the leash. In my beginner's classes I always ask for a show of hands: "Who here has a dog who's aggressive?" There aren't usually a lot of hands going up at this point, but some are, and that's good because, in this matter, admitting the problem really is halfway to a solution. Then I ask, "How many have a dog that is *not* aggressive?" More hands than before, but not always equal to class size minus the hands that went up the first time. Hmm, I say. Then, the final question: "How many think their dog MIGHT be aggressive?" Any hand that goes up this time gets a red flag in my mental notebook. I worry more about the people who think their dog might be a "teensy bit grouchy" than about the ones who can tell me straight, "Watch it: my dog might eat your arm." From the stranger-than-fiction file, I've heard such self-deluding equivocations as: "He might be aggressive, but only at night on the weekends." My all-time favorite, honest-to-Pete true story: "My dog smiles [read, bares his teeth!] and talks to me [read, growls!] when I try to take away his empty food bowl. He's just telling me he liked his dinner, isn't he?" A little denial can be a dangerous thing. Bottom line: If your dog has ever shown aggressive tendencies, or you think he MAY have issues that go beyond rambunctiousness, talk to a qualified dog trainer! Just as I would never endeavor to replace the fuel line in my car or perform hand surgery, you mustn't take on an aggressive dog alone.

If you have ruled out an aggression problem, I offer you the following.

The Checklist

Disclaimer: Any similarities to the checklists earlier in this chapter are entirely intentional. You're not experiencing déjà vu: this really is the same list from "Teaching 'Sit' " (page 68)—*almost*. I abbreviate, but feel free to go back and reread if anything doesn't seem familiar.

1. Start with a dog *ready* to train: Hungry, lonely, and/or bored.
2. Pick your motivator. In this case you need something that can be hidden in your closed fist. Those with toy-motivated dogs have to be a little creative. Got a small squeaky toy?
3. Be sure your dog is wearing the proper collar and a four- to six-foot leash.
4. Go to a quiet, distraction-free area.

5. The "down" command will be taught while you sit or kneel.

6. Your dog must already have a reliable "sit" command in his repertoire.

7. Your dog has no aggression issues that you are aware of. If you didn't read the "Danger, Will Robinson!" section on page 105, go back and check it out! And stop skipping sections!

Here we go.

THE FRONTAL, OR PRONE, DOWN—
TEACH THIS ONE FIRST!

1. Sit or kneel in front of your dog. He can be standing or sitting. Don't tell him which to do—it doesn't matter. (Besides, he doesn't even know a "stand" command!)

2. Show your dog the motivator. Then hide it in your closed *right* hand.

3. Put your right fist (with concealed motivator) up to the dog's nose and lower it slowly toward the ground (figure 13). By the way, this gesture will eventually become the hand signal for the down.

Figure 13. Right hand on ground, holding motivator.

4. With your hand firmly planted on the floor, wait and say nothing. If the dog is distracted, you can open your hand, show him the motivator again (to reset him), and then resume your vow of silence.

5. At this stage in training your dog probably knows the drill: He realizes you've got something he wants *and* that you want something from him in return. He *will* try to get the motivator. Expect lots of staring at your hand, maybe pawing it, maybe barking. Sometimes your dog will seem to practice some kind of Doggie Zen, sitting perfectly still and staring at your hand, as if trying to will the reward to come floating out to him. Not totally irrational: After all, he remembers that, when he sits, a reward of some sort usually materializes. I don't mind any response, as long as it's work related—his best guess at what will get him the reward. On the other hand, pulling at the leash to sniff the floor shows the wrong attitude and demands a redirection toward the motivator (aka "remember this?"). To redirect, bring your hand up to your dog's nose, open your hand briefly, and when you see recognition on his face (*there* it is!), close your hand and put it back on the ground. Dogs who stare off into space may not be distracted. Sometimes the staring is a reaction to the stress produced by this guessing game. (Learning is stressful!) The good news is that once the dog tries all the "wrong" behaviors he'll have only the correct one left to try. So be patient and have a little faith. If your dog exhibits stress, remember to keep your sessions short and upbeat. In the case of distraction, however, stress induced or not, your course is the same. Refocus him on the motivator and hang in there.

6. At some point your dog will tire of this wheedling and realize he should lie down. To comply, he must go all the way: elbows touching the ground, butt lowered, *not* up in the air. When he's got it right, your

response should be "Yes!" followed immediately by the opening of your hand to surrender the treat. If you're motivating with a toy, you can have a little play session now, but be sure to hold on to the toy! Remember, the amount of praise and playtime should be pegged to the type of dog you have: exuberant for the one who is laid back or has low confidence, more subdued for the one who is hard driving or high flying. IMPORTANT: Remember to release your dog from the down with an "Okay." (As with a sit, you must make him break it before he can learn to hold it.)

From a standing position the ideal down occurs as a single fluid movement, with the dog simply collapsing backward. From the sitting position, however, he will "crawl" a few steps with his front legs into a down. Some dogs will also roll on their hips, and some will stay up on their haunches. Remember that elbows have to be touching the ground for a properly executed down.

7. Repeat the preceding steps, noticing how quickly your dog flings himself into a down in order to get the reward.

8. Now add your dog's name and the word "down." Hereafter, it will always be the same form, for example, "Sparky, down." The command is to be given in a pleasant but firm voice and *never* repeated.

Continue anywhere from five to fifteen minutes (with a break for playtime) making sure to quit while your dog still wants to train!

The next time you train, start in the same location but then move to another room. Remember: Knowing the command in the living room does not automatically mean knowing it in the bedroom. It will take a while for your dog to generalize to the rest of the house. When he has mastered that, you can take the show on the road. When he is indoor/outdoor certified, proceed to "Getting off the Chuck Wagon" (page 118), "Correcting the Down" (page 121), and "Distractions on the Side" (page 125).

But for Those of You Still on the Floor with a Now-Melted Cheese Stick in Your Fist . . .

You look familiar. Ah yes, you're the ones who were icing their arms after trying to teach the "sit" command, right? Not to worry. I have more to offer you than physical therapy! If you've done your due diligence, attempting to teach the down as described but have come up empty-handed (or rather with a fistful of cheese), try these further forms of persuasion.

If your dog assumes a "play position" (front end down, butt end up), reach over him with your left (non-motivator) hand and apply gentle pressure on his lofty rear. Sometimes a light pat will suffice. Sometimes you'll need a little more pressure, enough to avoid misunderstanding. You don't want him thinking: " 'Down' means front half down, so as to present my cute butt for a soothing little massage until I collapse in ecstasy!" The pat is a mild correction, and you should use just enough pressure to produce a sensation your dog will prefer to avoid.

If your dog doesn't lie down at all, it's time to get physical. Lucky for you, the very next section is about . . .

The Physically Induced Down: Sweeping Your Dog off His Feet!

First, a reality check: It's no shame if your dog needs to be physically maneuvered into a down (or a sit, or various other behaviors). Every dog has his own needs, and in the end, when he is doing a solid down-stay at your son's baseball game, no one will ask whether you taught your dog that one using food or a gentle tackle. (They may ask, "What fabulous book did you use to train that superb dog!?" I leave the answer to your fair-minded discretion.) Before getting physical, be certain that you have given the motivator method a chance to work and that you have attempted it when your dog was in a training frame of mind: hungry, lonely, and/or bored. Try it for a week, once a day, in five- to fifteen-minute sessions, depending on your dog's endurance. But if you've taken your best shot with the motivator and haven't gotten the desired down, try this:

1. Nothing in your hand. You'll need both hands for this one!
2. Sit or kneel facing the dog.
3. Give the "down" command preceded by his name, and point to the ground with your right hand (this gesture will become the hand signal eventually).
4. Count a second or two ("one–one thousand").
5. If there is no down (as likely there isn't if you are still reading this), apply downward pressure to the leash and with your left hand across your dog's shoulder blades start applying pressure down and back (figure 14), increasing slowly until you see . . .
6. . . . your dog drop back into a down with a single fluid motion. Keep your hand on his shoulders (so he can't bounce back up!). As soon as he hits the ground, say, "Yes!" and release with "Okay." Depending on your dog's type, you may have either a big or low-key celebration.

Figure 14. Hand on shoulders applying downward pressure.

7. If your dog still won't go down, use both hands. If that doesn't work, use your left to push and the right to sweep his front paws gently out from under him and toward you (figure 15). Continue applying shoulder pressure with your left hand during the sweep. Remember, as soon as he hits the ground, say, "Yes!" and release with "Okay."

8. Repeat the maneuver until the dog is downing with little or no pressure.

Now you can move your hands off his shoulders and onto the leash. (For those dogs who are still not going down of their own accord following a dozen or so attempts at each of these techniques, try this next method, which involves leash and collar pressure.)

Facing your dog, hold the leash with both hands. Your right hand is on top, the pinkie near the snap, knuckles facing forward, thumb holding the leash. Your left hand is holding the leash under the right, in the same fashion. Your right pinkie is pressing on the leash making it taut and providing a fulcrum. This is reining position. If your dog does not obey the

Figure 15. Sweeping front legs out while pressing shoulders down.

"down" command, you will apply pressure on the leash down and toward him, aiming for the space between his front legs (figure 16). Do not tug or jerk. You want constant pressure, slowly increased until the dog chooses the correct response. *Note:* Be sure your dog has a suitable collar on! If he doesn't, consider an "upgrade" (from your point of view, not his!) to one that can give you more leverage.

Keep in mind that very high-energy, willful, and confident dogs can be the slowest to recognize that mastering this most submissive of behaviors is not optional. I've trained some that required some mighty pressure once I'd resorted to the leash and collar. I've also observed some who were so quick to respond to the leash that it was clear, in retrospect, they had not been given enough time to learn by the food/toy method. Often it turns out that the dog was not primed to train: His tummy was happy, or he'd been petted or played with all day. The motivator approach will work only under conditions when your dog's basic individual urges have not been gratified. In that case, even a high flier could be all too glad to do the down on a dime. Always err on the side of giving the motivator another chance, of trying it too many times rather than

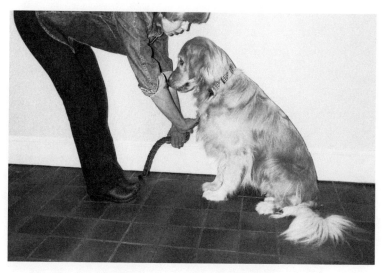

Figure 16. Applying downward leash pressure.

too few. As a rule, the most efficient and enjoyable (for both of you!) learning is always cooperative, rather than dictatorial, so the escalation to correction and physical maneuvering should be deferred until it's clear the command won't be learned any other way.

TEACHING THE CURLED DOWN

The curled down is one to use when you want to leave your dog in a down-wait. The checklist is the same as for the frontal down, except that you will be standing and your dog will begin by sitting at your left side in heel position (see scary italic text at the beginning of the "Curled Down" section on page 104). If you have a small dog or a puppy, you may kneel as long as you are otherwise conforming exactly to a standing heel position.

1. Show your dog the motivator. Whether food or a toy, it must be small enough to hide in your right fist.
2. Place the fist in which you've concealed the motivator up against the dog's nose and lower it very slowly toward the ground. Figure 13 on page 107 shows where your fist should end up if your dog will be downing from a sit, just slightly ahead of the dog.
3. Wait, and say nothing. Keep your hand firmly planted, unless you need to refocus the dog. Your dog may well remember this routine from the frontal-down lesson and go down without needing much effort on your part. If so, proceed to step 5. If not, wait until he does the down. Remember the elbows!
4. From the "*Why Didn't You Say So in the First Place?*" Department . . . Those of you who resorted to a physical method in the frontal down will need to do so with the curled down, too. (There is no motivator-based learning from the earlier lesson to build on here.) So, with your left hand across his shoulders, say your dog's name and "curl," and sweep his front

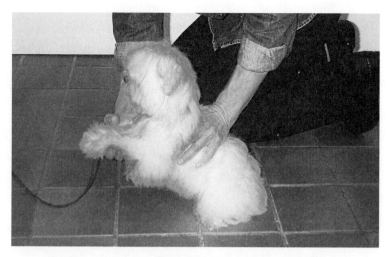

Figure 17. Gently sweeping front legs into a down position.

legs out from under him with your right hand (figure 17). If your dog is a large breed or a resistant type, you may need to put pressure on his right side by leaning (left) into him (figure 18). In any case, you must physically enforce the curl all the way. Simply waiting for him to happen upon the right idea, rewarding him at just the right moment of compliance,

Figure 18. Sweeping feet out while leaning into large or resistant dog.

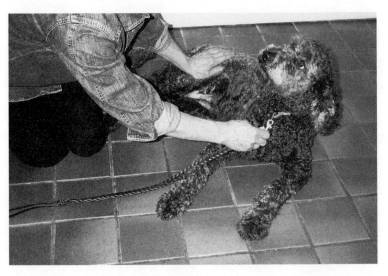

Figure 19. Left hand rolls dog's left hip into a "curled" down.

and getting him to repeat the whole routine enough times for the programming to stick—all that, I guarantee, would take more time than you have.

5. Once your dog is more than three-quarters of the way down, use your left hand to roll the dog's rear onto his left hip, *away* from you (figure 19). Keep your hand there so he doesn't roll back up into a crouch. Say, "Yes," praise him, and then release with an "Okay."

6. Once your dog is doing this down easily, with no resistance, add his name and the command "curl." Those of you who are physically helping your dog into a curl can skip this step because you've been saying "curl" from the beginning. It will always be "your dog's name" plus "curl." The command is to be given in a pleasant but firm voice and *never* to be repeated.

7. Continue anywhere from five to fifteen minutes (with a few breaks for playtime) and be sure to quit while your dog still wants to train!

The next time you train, try the down in the same location, but then move to another room. However well he may have the "down" command down in the kitchen, up in the bedroom may be a different matter. Always give him an opportunity to generalize the command to various situations.

Stand and Deliver

Those not married to a chiropractor or a massage therapist will certainly appreciate this next step.

All the scenarios for teaching down and curl, as you've probably noticed, involve your sitting, kneeling, or bending at the waist in order to lower the hand (containing the motivator) to the floor. However, now that your dog understands the position you want *her* to be in, she has to do it with you in the position that *you* want to be in, aka, upright. So the time has come for you to stand tall, but only if your dog has achieved a picture-perfect down (and curl) on command.

Note: If you had to use a more physical method to get your dog to lie down or curl, you can skip ahead to "Hands-Free Downing" (page 118). Don't make your dog (or yourself) the victim of low expectations: The picture-perfect down applies to your dog, too. But if your down sessions still look like wrestling matches, then you still have some work to do before recovering your well-aligned vertebrae.

First, have your dog do a frontal down in the usual manner, saying the command and lowering your hand to the ground. Praise, reward, and release. Life is good.

The next time you do it, stop your hand at six-to-twelve inches off the ground. Your dog may register some initial confusion, but understanding very well the verbal component, she will eventually go down. Continue with your hand in this position until she confidently goes down, without hesitation. Some dogs may get it after one or two times, some may require a few sessions. Be patient; it will happen. Praise, reward, and release. Life gets better all the time.

The next step is a giant one: Stand up. This time your hand will be two feet off the ground, which will require you to bend at the waist. But not for long. Once your dog has mastered the down with you standing and bending, lose the bend and stand tall. Life is beautiful.

Now that you have developed a reliable frontal down (still using a reward every time), you get to—okay, have to—repeat the whole process with the curl command. But since your dog understands that she has to work even when you're upright, she'll catch on to the curl much quicker.

HANDS-FREE DOWNING

Those of you who used the physical method to get your dog into the down or curl remember where we left off, right? For the frontal down you were using the reining position to put pressure on the leash. For the curled down, you were bending at the waist and sweeping your dog's feet out from underneath her. In either case, the prerequisites for *this* section are A) a dog who does a down with little to no resistance, and B) a human who's sick of bending at the waist.

Go to "Correcting the Down" (page 121). A slight deviation from those instructions: You may bend at the waist the first couple of times that you tell your dog to down, but after that you must stand upright. Follow the entire regimen and you'll have a dog who doesn't require you to bow to her before she lies down.

Once your dog is doing the command reliably with the food/toy motivator, take the show on the road. Then proceed with the round of distraction variations followed for the sit before you try . . .

GETTING OFF THE CHUCK WAGON

(Author's note: information from pages that your dog probably ripped out of the sit section, thoughtfully recapped for your convenience)

Those of you using food and toys, pay close attention! Those of you who used the physical method may take a twenty-minute nap.

Just as with the "sit" command, you'll notice after a few sessions that your dog understands the command "down." You'll know this because he automatically lies down, whether or not you have anything in your hand to offer him. Now we move on to random reinforcement. If you need a review of this concept, see page 78. To begin this phase, I give the reward for the first, the third, and the fifth downs. In the next round I'll give it on the first, the fifth, and the twelfth. "Random" means random: Don't follow a predictable pattern! Low-confidence dogs may need more time to be weaned off the treats; dogs with a really high food/play drive can wean relatively fast. Your objective is to make your dog's compliance totally independent of the food or toy. However, the goal is not to make obedience a thankless job. Every time your dog obeys, praise him (according to his type and needs) with "Good job," "Aren't you smart," etc., petting him and making him feel like the best dog in the world before you release him with "Okay." You just aren't handing out the food. Your dog's likely initial response? You know it:

NO COOKIE, NO DOWNIE!

That's the psychological barrier beyond which random reinforcement is designed to move your training.

Your relationship with your dog has to be based on a solid foundation of training, play, and love expressed through physical interaction but also by your reliably meeting his basic needs. In return, your dog gives you not only his love, but his obedience. This is the most important thing for him to understand, and which only proper training can instill: If you tell him do something, he must do it! If you've used a treat to teach him how to do something, he has learned only half the lesson until he figures out that the treat is not to be expected. The quid pro quo of his obedience is not a cheese stick or a rubber duck; rather it is your love and devotion to his well-being, in which he may place his utmost trust. The more worthy of that trust you are, the more reliably your dog will obey. But every good dog makes mistakes, and that's why we have corrections.

Remember: A correction is called for when a dog *who understands the command* is *choosing* not to obey, foolishly imagining he has a choice. While never abusive, the correction is something your dog wants to avoid. For sensitive dogs it may be a quiet "ah-ah" said without harshness.

Ah-ah: The Power of a Word

What's "ah-ah" to a dog? Really you could just as well be saying "grapefruit" for all he cares. It has no meaning until there is some sort of reinforcement (positive or negative) behind it. A fairly sensitive dog (most, actually) who hears "ah-ah" will usually stop and turn toward the sound. If that turn causes the dog to stop the incorrect behavior *and* the owner remembers to praise the dog for doing the correct thing at that specific moment, then the dog's understanding of the word "ah-ah" becomes "Stop what you are doing immediately." Many "ah-ah" utterers program this command without even realizing it, hence some of the mystique of those magic grunts. I'm an "ah-ah" advocate because I hate to say "no"—for many reasons (ask my parents!), but mainly because there isn't a person on the planet who can say "no" to a misbehaving dog without betraying at least a hint of anger. Dogs fear anger, ignore it, or are amped up by it, and all of those responses are bad for your training. However, if some dog is attacking you, then by all means, try a very angry "NO!" and pray that something in his miserable past tells him to be afraid!

For the rambunctious dog, correction may be a substantial tug on the leash. A dog with a more moderate temperament will need, well, something moderate, and training depends on finding the level of correction that will get his attention without hurting him (actual pain, psychological or physical, being not instructive but discouraging, even damaging). The point is not to punish, only to communicate that your dog's response to the command was unsatisfactory. Of course—and I can't over-stress this—correction is meaningful only to dogs who under-stand commands in the first place and haven't been spooked by some sight or sound they aren't trained to ignore.

CORRECTING THE DOWN—ANY DOWN— CURLED OR IN FRONT

If your dog completely understands the down command and isn't downing as taught or is downing too slowly, or is refusing to go down because you are not holding a toy or a cookie, bear in mind *who* it is at the end of the leash and what manner of correction makes sense for him.

First, a quick review of the pop: a tug on the leash ranging from mild to sharp. Use the minimum effective force. Make sure the leash is loose (taut leash = tug-of-war, no corrective effect). Before attempting this correction on your dog, practice popping on something sturdy so that you learn to pop without emotion. Angry? *No.* Decisive? *Yes!*

After an effective correction, double your normal praise. Release with "Okay" and begin again.

Let's run through the mechanics of a correction in the case of a frontal down. *Note:* From this point on, you will be telling your dog to sit before telling him to down. This ensures that he is attentive to you and is in the correct position (in front of you or at your side) before you begin.

Standing in front of your sitting dog and holding the leash (attached to your dog!), say his name and, without bending at the waist, say, "Down." If your dog starts going down but gets distracted by, say, an air molecule and stops, give him a mild pop, pulling toward the ground (figure 20).

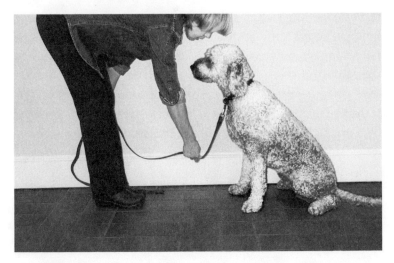

Figure 20. Correcting a refusal to "down" with a mild pop on leash.

- If he looks back at you and then lies down, say, "Yes!" then praise ("Good dog"), and release ("Okay").
- If a mild pop gets you a burp or a long stare but no down, your dog may have mistaken your message for an insect. Give him a stiffer pop the second time, but without repeating the command.
- If he goes down, say, "Yes!" then praise ("Good dog"), and release ("Okay").
- In the case of a curled down, your start position would be you, upright, with your dog sitting at your left side, both of you facing the same direction. Remember to substitute the word "curl" for "down" (figure 21).
- The pop, if needed, is the same.

"Pop Three Times"

If you have popped your dog three times, sharpening the tug with each try, if you have come to the end of your leash, so to speak, and think the next tug would be unproductively rough, it could be time to stop and re-examine the situation. Ask yourself: Have I taught the down thoroughly enough? Did my dog in fact show that he understood it in a variety of set-

Figure 21. Position for correcting a refusal to "curl."

tings? Perhaps some confusion has developed in his head as to what "down" really means. If there is even a *remote* chance of such uncertainty go back and retrain for a few days. This is not the end of the world! One step backward is sometimes necessary before you can take two forward. When it comes to corrections, which are strong signals, thus harder to deprogram, err on the side of caution. It's better to retrain a dog who is just feeling his oats than to correct a dog who is confused.

If you still don't get a down, this time apply *steady* pressure on the leash in the direction of the pops and physically push your dog into a down. If this is your first attempt at a physically induced down, you may want to go back to the section on the technique on page 110. The physicality you may have been able to skip when you were first training may now be necessary for remedial purposes if your dog is refusing to acknowledge what he has shown himself to have learned. (There is no roadblock he can erect that you can't bypass!) If need be, show him what it feels like to be swept off his feet! When he complies, say, "Yes!", offer praise ("Good down"), and release ("Okay").

For the Hydraulic Downers in Your Life

If "down" inspires your dog to set like the sun, you need to speed him up. As with the slo-mo sitter, the slow downer's sluggishness could suggest either a confidence problem or a power struggle, or it could just be his style. The more you train, the better your sense of what the situation might be. Always start out assuming he's innocent until you prove him guilty. If confidence is the issue, more practice should speed him up. If he is not in the downing vein or has decided for some reason to take his stand against this objectionable command, vee have vays of refreshing his memory of who's the boss:

- The "I Got You!" game. When your dog begins his maddeningly slow descent, quickly but gently reach out and push on his shoulders or butt. If he hits the deck immediately, praise, and release with "Okay." Repeat. This is an eloquent little message that should inspire your dog to get down *before* you lay your hand on him. ("If she's gonna push me anyway, I might as well beat her to it, and maybe score some points. Hey, didn't I used to get a little string cheese for this once upon a time?")
- The correction option. Start out exactly as prescribed for correcting the down, but in this case when you enforce the correction on a slow down, you DO repeat the command "down." Another rare exception to the nonrepetition rule, with the usual risk: If your dog in any way interprets this correction to mean he's making a mistake by lying down, you are sunk! That's why you must correct and repeat the command in perfect synchronization. If you do repeat "down" at the very moment you pop, he will understand that he was doing the right thing at the wrong speed. As soon as he gets up to speed, stop repeating the command—no one will be any the wiser.

Continue working on the down (and curl, but not in the same session) until just before your dog starts looking fatigued or bored. After a few successful downs, end the session in whatever way is most gratifying for your type of dog, from elaborate praise for the wallflower to crate time for the wall climber (see page 83 in the "Sit" section if your memory needs jogging). The right cool-down is critical to success, and it won't always be exactly the same. Remember that your dog will constantly be evolving during the training process. It's your job to know who he is and what he needs from week to week.

Final, very important note: If your correction meets with any manner of aggression—be it a growl, a bite, or anything in between—you need the counsel of a professional trainer or behaviorist before continuing to train. The reason for such behavior is generally *not* the pop on the leash. Your dog may well have other issues, which, left unaddressed, will continue to manifest themselves and increase in intensity.

DISTRACTIONS ON THE SIDE
(Oh, no, not this again!)

Yes, this again! But there's a bright spot: Since your dog has already assimilated the *concept* of distraction in relation to the "sit" and the "wait" commands, you will likely notice he can work through distractions more easily with the down. If you yourself haven't fully assimilated the distraction concept, you may want to have another look at "A Distracting Situation" on page 84. I'll spare you the "Loss of Innocence" (page 85) recap!

When introducing distractions, always bear in mind your dog's type: Depending on his drives, the same dog may be unfazed by a dozen tennis balls but lose his head completely at the sight of a dog cookie at his feet. If you notice a particular distraction is overwhelming, make it "smaller," so your dog can learn to cope with it gradually. If, for instance, you know your food-driven dog to be a cookie monster, try distracting him with some less irresistible food before trifling with his ultimate thrill. The point is to identify and increase his tolerance for distraction, not to blow a fuse—in him or you!

Here's an example of training the down with distractions:

Dog type: moderately toy driven
Distraction theater: living room
External stimulus: cookie, made for dogs

1. With dog on leash, owner puts the cookie on the ground six feet away, making sure dog knows it's there. (If your dog isn't eagle-eyed, feel free to point the cookie out to him.) Owner gives the command: "Blaze, down."

2. Blaze seems to have assumed an alias. Else, he has forgotten everything he knows about "down." He bolts to investigate the cookie. Is Blaze evil? Stupid? Spiteful? None of the above! He has simply made a mistake. Without making mistakes none of us would learn a thing. Now is not the moment for retribution but instruction.

3. Blaze's owner calmly (read: without anger or malice aforethought) walks over and *gently* takes him by the collar back to the starting point to physically enforce the down—decisively but without heat. As soon as Blaze has assumed the position, surrendering to the correction, he is saluted with praise ("Yes, goood dog") and released ("Okay").

4. On the second attempt of cookie distraction, it's a whole different ball game, right? Get real—this isn't television, and Blaze is not Lassie. Naturally he makes for the cookie yet again! If history has taught him anything, the owner knows by now not to surrender enough leash for Blaze to go the whole nine yards (okay, I said six feet) the second time. But that's not all the owner's learned: The first correction was ineffective. This time he tries a mild pop on the leash. This

gets Blaze's attention: A look of baffled innocence is promptly followed by a down. The owner praises and releases.

Now, suppose Blaze *hadn't* responded to the leash pop. The owner would try it again, and then a third time. If pops still made no difference, the only way forward would be backward. Escalating the correction past a third pop simply becomes another species of distraction. The only real choice is to reduce the distraction or reteach the behavior that the dog seemed to know when distractions were not present. It's always safer to give the dog the benefit of the doubt and assume he's over-whelmed or uncertain rather than obstreperous. You can always gradually increase the degree of distraction difficulty. In training with distractions, we look for consistency, not speed.

Once Blaze has mastered the cookie distraction, his under-standing of "down" must be tested under other distracting conditions. The dog must verify that he can do it wherever called upon: on a train, on a plane. In the house, with a mouse. "Down" means down here or there, everywhere, anytime. Run him through the range of likely scenarios: tykes on bikes, fly-ing balls, speeding cars, wet grass, exuberant strangers, and, if you live near a dairy, a grazing cow. The more eventualities you anticipate, the less likely you will be to witness an unex-pected flight of the cookie monster. And, of course, I don't have to remind you to repeat this whole procedure with your curl command, do I?

Now, Wait Just a Minute . . .

Or more like three seconds. That's probably the length of time your dog would remain in the down or curl position if you didn't release him. Now it's time to teach your dog to down and *wait*. And curl and wait. With distractions.

Go back to "Teaching 'Wait'" (page 92) and substitute the sit command for the down command. But remember to use your down correction (not the one for sit) if correction is needed. *Good News Alert:* You'll find that teaching the down and wait goes much faster (read: easier) than teaching the sit and wait. That's because your dog should have already mastered the concept of "wait" in the context of the sit command. Translation—your dog may sail through to a reliable down and wait. Which is terrific, because then I want you to go back through the entire process using the curl command.

A dog who can lie down on command: Impressive. A dog who can lie down on command and wait: Priceless.

"I REMEMBER SOMETHING ABOUT A DOWN HAND SIGNAL"

(Or, "Show me something my neighbor's dog can't do")

At this point you should have a dog who can do both types of down, even under some distracting circumstances. You have weaned him off constant rewards (food or toy) but continue to reward him at random for his compliance—so that he never knows just *which* down will be the "open sesame" that releases the cheese or rubber mouse from your fist. Your dog seems to have figured things out: He can't predict the reward and recognizes that obeying your command is not a matter of his choice (in fact, the very idea of "his choice" is starting to seem to him like crazy talk, bound to get him nothing but a pop on the leash). Have I described your situation? If not, I regret to inform you that you've got to follow the down drill for a little while longer. If, however, I paint a true picture (and it's certainly a pretty one!), it's time to reward *you* (for a change) with a little trick sure to make you look like one smooth dog owner. It's time to learn to give a command with nothing but your hand.

The "down" command that gets the hand signal is the prone down (aka the frontal down, which your dog does while facing you). Eventually you'll be standing far away from your dog, so he needs a signal he can see from a distance. (With the curled down you will always be standing next to your dog, so a hand signal is not practical.)

Remember your "wait" command? Left hand (like palming a basketball) placed just above the dog's eyes. The finished down signal will look similar, but you'll use your *right* hand, and you'll be standing not as near your dog, presenting your palm with fingers together and arm fully

Figure 22. Down hand signal.

extended (figure 22). For better visibility, you can adjust the angle of your arm to your body, depending on the height of your dog: For big dogs, you signal from on high (like driving an SUV), about shoulder level, forming a right angle with your chest (figure 23). For medium dogs, the signal is

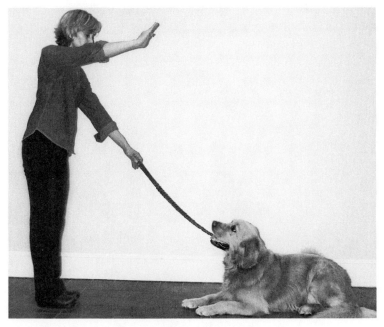

Figure 23. Down hand signal for large dogs.

Figure 24. Down hand signal for medium dogs.

given from somewhere between chest to waist level (figure 24). For small dogs, the angle is just great enough to show that your arm is slightly away from your body (figure 25). The signal itself is sort of like the universal stop sign, crisp and sharp, as you might see it given by a guard at a border

Figure 25. Down hand signal for small dogs.

checkpoint. If your signal is too limp or lazy, you'll get just that sort of response from the dog. The more decisive signal gets the quicker and more generally impressive down. Now, that's the *finished* look of the signal. How do we get there? As usual we start slow and build up. This command is best taught using food or a toy. I'll explain how you can teach it physically if that procedure becomes necessary, but it's learned much more quickly if you can use a motivator. Microwaved liver with garlic is especially recommended! Here we go:

1. You are either standing, sitting, or kneeling in front of your dog. He can be either standing or sitting.
2. Show him the motivator. ("Do I smell garlic?")
3. In your open right hand, hold the motivator a few inches above the dog's nose and say his name plus "down." See figure 26 for the exact hand position. Note that your thumb is holding the motivator, preventing the possibility of shoplifting.
4. Do not repeat the command. In fact, say nothing; just keep your hand up. If your dog is particularly

Figure 26. Holding motivator while giving down hand signal.

submissive you may avert your eyes so he isn't intimidated.

5. If he doesn't catch on after a reasonable time, start lowering your hand very slowly toward the ground, waiting a few seconds with every couple of inches to see whether the lightbulb goes on. It will, don't worry!

6. Finally he goes into a *correct* down. Your response, as always, should be praise ("Yes!") followed immediately by opening your hand and giving him the food. Then release: "Okay." If you're motivating with a toy, you can have a brief play session; just be sure to hold on to the toy!

7. Repeat the process, noting how quickly your dog flings himself into a down now that he understands how to get the reward. When he is descending almost before you can say "down," that's the ticket: Houston, we have recognition!

8. On the next attempt raise the signal about two inches. After five or six consecutive correct responses, raise it again. Continue this raising until you are signaling with your arm at an angle suited to your dog's size.

9. If you have been giving the signal while seated until now, switch to a kneeling position. Your dog should have no trouble adjusting to the difference, though you may find it a little tougher.

10. Once he is reliably responding to the signal you're giving on your knees, get up (if you can!) and start working the same routine while standing up straight, saying "down" once and lowering the arm incrementally until he obeys. (I say "straight," having noticed that people love to bend at the waist while giving the down signal. Rest assured: Dogs have keen eyesight. Adjusting the arm angle is more than enough help.)

11. Once you're giving the signal successfully while on your feet, it's time to start eliminating the verbal part

of the command. On every other attempt now, give the signal without saying "down." Stretch that to every third attempt, then every fifth, and so on. I continue to supply the word command on the first attempt in every session throughout the initial teaching phase. And just as the verbal command is being eliminated, so must the reward. Refresh your memory by reading "Getting off the Chuck Wagon" (page 118), if you must.

12. Now your dog knows a pure hand signal for a frontal down. Congratulations (to both of you)!

What if, after He Understands the Command, My Dog Ignores the Signal?

By now, you can probably guess that my advice will *not* be to repeat the command signal with more exaggeration, nor to scream at your dog until he obeys. If the dog was distracted and missed the gesture, try it again when you are sure he's focused. If, however, you think he just didn't feel like obeying, there's only one option. A dog who understands the meaning of the "down" signal but chooses to ignore it is asking for a correction.

1. Hold the leash in your left hand as you stand facing the dog (you do have your dog's attention, right?), and without verbal command, give the "down" signal with your right hand—a clean, crisp motion. (Remember the border guard: Your signal must say "I mean business," not "Gee, it sure would be nice if someone around here went down.")

2. If your dog doesn't respond, immediately give the leash a light pop with your signal (right) hand, pulling down and back between his front legs (figure 27). If your dog goes down, praise ("Good") and release ("Okay").

3. If your dog starts to down but gets distracted by an air molecule and sits instead, give him another pop (same strength), pulling toward the ground. Don't

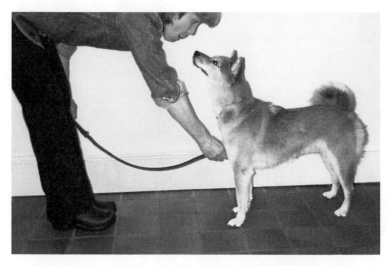

Figure 27. Popping leash down and between dog's front legs.

repeat the command signal. If this approach works, say, "Yes!", then praise ("Good down") and release ("Okay").

4. If he looks at you but does not go down, reset: Give the hand signal, and, this time, increase the pop intensity slightly, repeating at that pop level until he gets the message. (He will after a time. After all, he has been thoroughly trained to lie down on command, so this time the correction phase should go extremely quickly.) Keep working until your dog not only does a down on your hand signal alone, but also does it quickly and decisively. Continue five to fifteen minutes (with a few breaks for playtime).

If this process works, you've reached a milestone, with your dog obeying your commands on sight alone. Pretty nifty, and sure to impress friends and relatives. But don't start mailing out the party invitations just yet unless you plan on videotaping this feat and showing your guests the footage. All you've done is establish the behavior in the quiet solitude of your living room; it will be a whole different ball game (for the dog anyway) with a room full of gawkers. So, I'm afraid it's on to . . . distractions! I know: A dog owner's work is never done. But neither is a dog's. At least you can have a beer later. Anyway, the drill should be very familiar to both of you by now. A down with distractions: bikes, kids, automobiles, "heavy petters," wet grass, etc. He must do the down on a train or on a plane, near a bus and without a fuss. He must do the down here or there, anytime, anywhere. Distraction certification is especially important with the down's nonverbal command simply because, unless he is 100 percent focused on you, he'll miss the signal. If you give a "down" signal in the forest and the dog doesn't see it, was there something to see? You bet there was!

Un-leash Me, You Brute!

Ding Dong! That's the front door. You can tell by the manic scrabbling sounds of dog nails on the linoleum in the hallway (memo to you—clip dog's nails) that he's already beaten you to it. On the other side you hear your sister-in-law's darling little girls screaming in terror at the commotion inside. Taking after their mother, the kids are deathly afraid of dogs—hence, they are infrequent visitors. Your dog being a dog, the high-pitch of little girls' screams has amped him up into a hysteria. Your sister-in-law is now ringing the bell impatiently, while telling her kids in less-than-tender tones to "knock it off!" You need to get control over this situation, or head out the back door. Deciding to stay and face the music, you start looking for your dog's leash, the theory being that once you have it on him you can command him into the down position that you've been practicing so diligently. To canine-phobes, a dog in a down position is much less threatening, even less threatening then one in a sit. But wait, there's a fly in the ointment. Your kids, while playing at tying each other to a tree, left the leash in the backyard, which now leaves *you* up a tree. Calgon, take me away.

If only you had taught your dog to down (and curl) off leash. You didn't say "how?" did you? Then you would be totally busted, because I would know that you hadn't read "Look, Ma, No Leash!" (page 90), which outlines the entire process for the sit command. Review the procedure for teaching a sit command off leash. Substitute the down, curl and down hand signal for the sit command, and, if needed, the relevant corrections for those employed for the sit.

A Word to the Wise: Sit is the easiest off-leash command to teach (it's far easier to put a resistant dog into a sit than into a down); therefore if you haven't for some reason taught the sit off leash, do that first. Once your dog understands the idea of working away from you on a sit command, the down commands will go much quicker.

While I'm cracking the whip, I still want to give you (both) a pat on the back. You have done a lot so far. Now you have a dog who does a frontal and a curled down, and can also go down on sight alone! I'm almost tempted to end the chapter on such a high note. But you'll be glad I didn't, when you realize the next command is too good to wait for. I speak of the dream-dog "come when called" command.

TEACHING "HERE"

(Not "Commear"; "Come on"; or "Come-on-now-sweetum-get-over-here!" Just "Here!")

Definition of a perfect here: Dog and owner are on a walk through the woods. The dog, not yet thoroughly trained, is on a retractable leash, sniffing and darting his way along the path. Suddenly, the dog gets the scent of something great (a rabbit?!) and takes off after it. The owner calls out, "Shelby, here!" Shelby freezes, and instantly wheels around to make a fast beeline back to the owner. Once there, he sits before his master and awaits the next command. Following praise and release, they continue on their solitary way.

This scene will be familiar to many of you—up until the part where "Shelby freezes, and instantly wheels around," etc. While individual results may vary, more than likely your current version ends with something like this: Shelby bolts after his quarry at a speed to suggest you will see neither hide nor hair of him again. Owner (that's you) races after him until realizing she couldn't run a quarter mile to save her life; she plants herself at the next clearing, leans against a tree ("Hmm, I hope this isn't poison oak"), trying to catch her breath and praying the thoughtless brute will find her eventually. Substituting for the praise part is a string of expletives as she limps back to the car, *with* the dog if she is among the lucky ones.

Good thing I didn't end this book with that neat hand-signal climax, don't you think?

"Here" vs. "Come"

As I suggested a little earlier, the word for the behavior we're looking for is "here"—*not* "come." You may think that I'm just trying to be difficult, or different just to be different. After all, what is in a word? If anything, "come" rolls more easily off the tongue than the aspirative/guttural noise that produces "here." And anyway, isn't "come," in all it's imploring combinations, a much more common command? My point exactly! All his days, your dog has been hearing "Come"; "Com'ere"; "Come *on*"; "Come to Mommie, please," to say nothing of various phonetically similar but totally unrelated words: "*Comm*ercial! Let's get a snack . . . *kum*quats?" "Sorry, that's all we've got. *Come* on, let's get *com*fy. The show's about to *comm*ence." Okay, not the most realistic dialogue, but I hope you'll take my point: "Come" is a sound your dog has, for the most part, learned to tune out. In addition, even if you have attempted to attach a command expectation to that utterance, chances are it was never properly taught and enforced, much less reinforced—and certainly not to the point of freezing a dog in mad flight after a rabbit. (I presume you *do* want such a command in your arsenal, correct?) So in the best case, "come" means nothing to your dog. In the worst, it has bitter associations as something he hears just before a verbal or physical (or both!) correction for making a he-has-no-clue-what mistake in executing something he was never properly taught. Yes, "come" is a wonderfully melodious, comely word. But let's make a point never to use it in training!

It's much easier to teach with a new word than to rescue a familiar or ambiguous one from the background noise of over-use. The raspier word "here" is the sound that your dog will learn means "drop everything and return to me." Let the kids say "come" when they are calling the dog. Kids tend to repeat commands, and not enforce them (wonder where they get *that* from), so unless you plan to rigorously train your children to train the dog, let them have "come" while you reserve "here" strictly for your own communication with your canine part-ner. If you do, you'll find that a word can speak volumes!

The Promise

I am now formally requesting that you swear on your dog's head to follow these Very Important Rules:

1. I will never give my dog the command "here" in the training stages unless he is wearing a leash and a collar.
2. I will never give my dog (attired as per Rule #1) the command "here" unless I am able and willing to enforce it.
3. I will never let my dog loose in an unconfined area until he has been thoroughly taught and proofed on his "here" command and, even then, not if I can help it!
4. I will buy this book for all my relatives this holiday season!

Oh, all right, so my subliminal messaging needs some work! But the first three rules are reasonable and crucially important to the success of the "here" command.

The Checklist

Another day, another recap.

1. Start with a dog that is *ready* to train: hungry, lonely, and/or bored. Pick your motivator. If food works for

you, it must be some morsel that the dog can eat in three seconds or less.

2. Be sure your dog is wearing a collar and a leash that is at least six feet long. You will also need a twenty-six-foot retractable leash and a fifty-foot light line as you progress in the exercise (see page 42).

"Here" we go.

The Easy Way: With a Lure

1. Let your dog know you have the motivator in your right hand (we'll use food as an example). Let him smell it, lick it, or even have a little nibble.

2. With the leash in your left hand, walk briskly backward, away from the dog, with your right arm extended toward him and say his name followed by "here" (figure 28). Be sure that your arm is level with your dog's nose. A small dog won't know you have a treat if you're holding it too high, and in some cases you may have to bend at the waist.

Figure 28. Briskly backing up, motivator close to dog's nose.

(A word about backing up: WATCH WHERE YOU'RE GOING! I have had more than a few students enthusiastically ambling in reverse and praising their dogs, only to trip over a stray shoe and land right on their tailbones. The dogs enjoy this tremendously, but it's not essential to the lesson or even recommended.)

3. As your dog starts moving toward you, praise her lavishly and keep backing up quickly.
4. After a few more steps, stop retreating, but start swinging your arm down toward your body until your knuckles are touching your knees or whatever part of the front of your body is level with your dog's sight line.
5. When your dog is all the way to you, let her nibble at the food (figure 29).
6. While she is nibbling, slowly take your left hand (yes, I know you still have the leash in that hand; do it anyway) and hook a finger in her collar. At the very moment your finger hooks the collar, release the food into her mouth and praise her. *Hooking the collar*

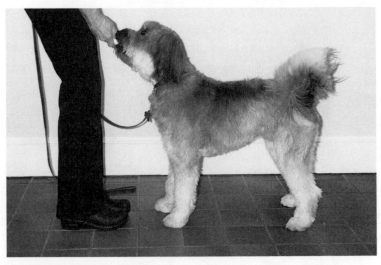

Figure 29. Hand is against leg while dog is nibbling food.

correctly—a quick finger action—is extremely impor-
tant. (It will not do to grab the collar.) If you're sloppy
about it, your dog will run away as soon as she has the
lure and before you've got her, which results in dissociat-
ing the hook sensation from the treat. The trick is for
your dog to understand that, when you have her by the
collar in this particular way, after having said "here,"
something good (her cookie) will come of it!

7. Release with "Okay."
8. Since your dog already knows "sit," you can slip that in before the collar hook, after a little practice. When she gets all the way into you, tell her to sit, letting her have a nibble of the food. Then hook her, surrender the lure, praise, and release.

Next time you practice this, alter the frame of spatial reference. You may need to start small (for instance, backing up in a
different direction) before switching to another room, then
outside, and so forth. Otherwise your dog might very reason-
ably assume, "Hmm, this 'here' thing must be my new kitchen
duty."

The Still-Pretty-Easy Physical Way: "Here" Without a Lure

Instead of luring, you'll simply say your dog's name plus
"here" and then back up. The more lively your retreat the
more lively will be his advance. Once he's headed in your
direction, remember to praise, praise, praise! Even without the
promise of a treat, the fact that he's attached to the leash as
you're backing up will—by the immutable laws of physics—
assure that he will soon be pulled toward you. Trouble is,
"pulled toward you" and "coming toward you" are two
slightly different concepts. He really isn't coming of his own
free will. So the physically induced way will take longer to
program. When he's moving in your direction, start drawing
in the leash (so as to limit his options) and praise him profusely
when he arrives (so as to make his cooperation seem like some-

thing good that he's discovered). Again, a food or toy motivator is more dramatically effective, but praise eventually does suffice. And of course, what training would be complete without . . .

The Bite

"Man bites dog": That's news, right? Don't worry, we're not out to make headlines. There isn't any actual biting involved here, either by you or your dog: "Bite" is just another word for "correction." After a while your dog understands that, when you say his name plus "here," that means come, and on the double. As no one's perfect, you'll also need to show him what happens if he doesn't comply with your command. It isn't just a matter of rules. "Here," like "down," is meant to be one of those emergency-break commands that could one day save your dog from stepping on broken glass or running in front of a speeding car. You must have zero tolerance for anything less than perfect compliance. But rather than waiting for a disaster to assess the limits of his learning, we're going to force an error with distraction.

Distractions are introduced very early in this exercise. As always, choose particular ones based on knowledge of your dog—his own Achilles' heel, the curves he's most likely to be thrown in your shared world. And start with the easy ones, working your way up to the difficult; at first, just enough distraction to force an error, but not enough to overwhelm him entirely. The possibilities, as you know by now, are endless, from the voices of strangers to the surprise appearance of food to the kids' saying, "Where's kitty?" to the neighbors' dog barking at four a.m. to the ever-tricky, wet grass. And so, without further ado:

1. Start as you would teaching "here"—leash, collar, food, or toy.
2. While still holding on to the leash, launch distraction.
3. When he has walked away and has his back to you, call him with his name plus "here."

In this correction, it's important that he be looking away from you, not merely because it's harder for you to administer a pop when staring into his big brown eyes. The point is for him to conclude that your verbal command was a warning to him of impending danger, and when he chose to ignore the warning, this danger—not you, his beloved owner—"bit" him on the neck. You can well imagine that, if he's looking when you pop him, it will be pretty difficult to put this one over on him. That said, there's no denying that there will be times when you'll have to pop him even when his gaze is not averted. To be caught in the act here is still the lesser of two evils (preferable to his concluding that the "here" command is optional), but if possible do arrange it so that you can avoid being seen as the popper. If he doesn't respond immediately, count "One–one thousand." That is the amount of time he has to think it over. If he comes, start trotting backward, and praising. If not . . .*

4. . . . Pop goes the leash. The pop should be level with his back (a small dog popped upward might wind up airborne—not good! Also, make sure there is slack in the leash, otherwise you'll be dragging rather than popping). If the correction works, start quickly backing up and praising exuberantly.
5. Tell your dog to sit when he gets to you, and hook a finger under his collar. Once he's hooked, surrender the treat, praise, and release.

When you set him up to do it again, you may notice reluctance on your dog's part to wander off. That's normal—once bitten, twice shy. It's also progress, meaning you can and must try a more difficult distraction—change of scene, sirens, sprinklers, what have you. You can't overteach the "here" command. At the same time there is an important distinction between the dog's understanding that the command is nonnegotiable and his concluding that there is no right place to be but by your side always—as he will conclude initially. The objective is for the dog to understand that he can go wherever he likes so long as he keeps an ear out for that special, inviolable word: "here."

When he responds correctly three times in a row, you need to change location and distractions. Or you need to come back and do some more work later. When you notice that you can no longer distract your dog on your six-foot leash (aka, he always comes when you say, "Here"), you can move ahead to page 149, "Coming When Called on a Twenty-Six-Foot Leash." For those still having some problems, however, here's a bit of diagnostic help.

THINGS THAT CAN AND WILL GO WRONG

My dog won't come!

Is your dog confused? Are you sure you made sufficient attempts with a lure? If not, go back and reteach, being extra-careful about the dog's readiness to train: hungry, lonely, and/ or bored. A suitably primed dog taught correctly ten minutes a day for three days is extremely likely to grasp the concept.

Consider, too, the quality of your pop. Is it hard enough? By now you should have a clearer sense of what level of correction is not injurious but still impossible for your dog to ignore. Is it substantial enough to count as something your dog would work to avoid? If your pop is more a suggestion than an order, your dog may not mind "taking it on the chin" in order to continue with what he's doing. For the namby-pamby poppers among my students, I always repeat that a pop, though uncomfortable, hurts a lot less than getting hit by a car.

My dog comes slowly.

As always, quality of obedience depends on depth of instruction. The "here" command, like skating's double lutz, has its precise criteria, and there's a lot that can go wrong between execution and a perfect ten. The dog must come *immediately,* without sniffing the ground, in a straight line, on the double, and sit in front of you. When a dog comes slowly, that's a partially incorrect response to the command, and an indication that we have work to do. How to communicate that speed is of the essence? After I've called "here" to him, if he seems to be taking his sweet time, I'll give him a *little* pop, followed immediately by a another command: "hurry." I know, I know, I've just gotten through telling you not to be seen popping! It's more bending than breaking the rule, and besides, just because he sees you popping, he doesn't assume all pops come from you when he's not looking. (Trust me: Dogs don't usually connect the dots that well.) While you're hurrying him along, be quick yourself about backing up. A slow retreat is no way to inspire urgency in your dog. If you back up quickly, chances are your dog will pick up the pace, too. (If not, there's always another pop where the first one came from.) But, a word of caution about hasty retreats: If you know your dog to have a strong play drive, then zipping backward will very likely provoke him to overtake and run you over. So be careful in reverse, but in any case, don't forget to praise, as long as your training does not become a hit-and-run.

My dog starts to come when I call him, but then gets distracted and wanders off.

This situation is like having an eight-year-old boy in the house. You call upstairs: "David, come down for dinner!" You hear the sound of feet on the stairs, but soon you notice: no David. Five minutes pass, and you go looking, only to find him lying on the couch, reading a comic book. "What are you doing?!" you ask, rhetorically. "Nothing," he says (using the eight-year-old's term for all activities not related to video games). "I said, 'Come down for dinner!'" you repeat. "Okay," the boy huffs, as if hearing you for the first time. This kind of thing happens with dogs, too. Fortunately, in the canine case, you can refocus your dog with a pop on the leash and reinforce the direction with gratefully received praise.

My dog comes halfway to me and just stops.

If you have ever reached for your dog in anger or met him halfway with praise or a dog cookie, then you are part of the problem, not the solution! I know you meant no harm, were only trying to say, "That's it, Spike, keep coming," but all Spike heard was approval for his having stopped midway. Even if you swear up and down that you never did such a misleading thing, the remedy for chronic halfway comers is the same: Go back to teaching the "here" command, and stay at it for a week.

If your dog knows what's expected (has demonstrated a capacity to come all the way when called) and is therefore engaging you in a power struggle ("Learn this!"), correction rather than reteaching is in order, and you can pop him again while you're backing up. Maybe your pops need to be slightly stronger and better amplified with the help of a more substantial collar. Beware that, as with training all the submissive behaviors (down and here), this can escalate into a war of wills. It's a war worth the fighting: You must have a reliable recall command whatever the cost. A dog who won't consistently roll over is something you can live with—your choice; the danger to a dog half-trained to come is too terrible to speak of.

My dog comes all the way and then runs right past me!

Eventually your dog will understand that he'll never get a cheeseburger and fries driving past you, but we must discourage the behavior before that. Say nothing, turn to face the direction in which he is running, and give a pop, as though he has failed to come when you called him. Actually he has failed, only partially, but there is no partial credit: "Here" means "Come to where I am exactly," not "Have a look-see hereabouts, and be on your merry way." After the second pop, back up as you would after an initial correction. Coil up the leash as he comes in, so that you can enforce a "sit" command when he gets to you.

My dog comes but offers only a crooked sit, or none at all.

Coil the leash as your dog approaches. When he is one to two feet away, hold the gathered leash with your left hand in the center of your body. Use your right hand, palm open and down, to create a pivot point at the other end of the leash by the bolt (figure 30). Pressure up and into you with your right hand while pulling the gathered end toward you as you say, "Sit." This gives the dog very little leash so that he can't be that far off center. And for those dogs who aren't sitting because they don't care to (a judgment call, I know), you may use a pop instead of reining the leash up and in. As always, the key is to ascertain *why* your dog isn't performing correctly. Is it canine or human error?

Figure 30. Creating a pivot point to pressure up and into a sit.

My dog jumps up and knocks me over when she comes, but otherwise she comes to me perfectly!

Well, she's not coming perfectly, then, is she? "Here" means a number of nonnegotiable things, and very high on the list is "Sit in front of me when you get here." If you think momentum is the problem, try telling your dog to sit when she gets to within five feet of you. Some dogs come in so fast, they can scarcely process information while on the move; you may need to give your dog extra time to hear and act on the "sit" command. If, however, she has demonstrated perfect comprehension of what is expected but simply enjoys jumping up on you (or hearing that thump when you hit the ground), then by all means pop her as you say, "Sit!"

Finally: My dog growls and bares his teeth when I try to enforce the "here" command.

Always keep an eye out for pathological aggressive tendencies and err on the side of caution, seeking counsel from a professional.

Once you have a dog who comes to you on a six-foot leash and you have ironed out any "technical" problems, work through the usual variety of distractions suited to your dog, lifestyle, vicinity, and so forth. If your dog is *not* 100 percent reliable about coming when called on a leash, with distractions, *do not* proceed to the next exercise! Go back and continue working!

You have now arrived at the stage where you put your command to the test and work on a longer-than-six-foot leash. The leash of choice is a twenty-six-foot retractable leash called a flexi leash. A long leash allows me to give the dog greater freedom and to test the reliability of my "here" command. Most dogs with very little training will come when called at a distance of six feet (the length of the leash you were using when you initially taught the command). However, when dogs feel they are out of "correcting" distance, they become deaf! Not clinically deaf, of course, it's more of a selective hearing disorder. By the way, please don't be lulled into a false sense of security when your dog comes to you on a short leash—even through the most harrowing of distractions! Your command is not complete. The majority of the times you will need your dog to come to you is *not* when he is on a leash, six feet away. The times you will really need him to come are when he's far away and *off* leash! That said, let's move on to . . .

COMING WHEN CALLED ON A TWENTY-SIX-FOOT LEASH

You really need to have a flexi for this section (there are other brands, but I prefer flexi). If you don't have one or can't find one, then you need to buy a twenty-six-foot-long leash and use that. You won't have the luxury of a leash that retracts as the dog comes into you, so you'll have to do some major coiling of the line, but hey, as long as you're training your dog, I'm happy!

As you already know from the early stages of teaching the "here" command, you have to have a distracted dog in order to get a correction in. And as you also know, you must start out with an easy distraction and work up to difficult one. Since you're so smart and know all this stuff, let's get on with the training! (For those of you who aren't savants and need a refresher, go back to page 142 and review "The Bite" section on distractions.)

Part One

- Your dog is on his flexi, hopefully wandering off some-where.
- When your dog is distracted, and his back is to you, call his name and say, "Here."
- If there is no response, mentally count, "One—one thousand." That is the amount of time he has to make a decision whether to come.
- If he still does not come to you, give a pop on the leash. *(Flexi owners: There is a special method of popping on a flexi that I'll explain here, called the Press-Pop-Release [PPR] technique. First, press on the large black button— the brake—and hold it down. Next pop the leash— remember to have slack in it, or all you'll be doing is drag-ging the dog. After your pop, release the brake, and, as the dog comes toward you, the line will retract into the plastic handle. If at any point you need to correct again,*

repeat the same steps. IF YOU FORGET TO PUSH THE BRAKE DOWN AND HOLD IT WHEN YOU POP, YOU WILL HIT YOURSELF IN THE FACE. And with plastic-surgery costs being what they are today, you'd best practice that Press-Pop-Release drill a bit before you try it on your dog.

- Back up and praise when your dog is coming to you. During this phase, you need only to hook his collar every other or every third time, just to remind him that holding his collar is a good thing.
- Praise and release. You can give him a treat the first time and then every fifth time or so. By the end of this step you'll have weaned your dog totally off the food (or his toy!), so remember to praise extra-enthusiastically!

Try, try again. Your dog will probably be a bit surprised at first that the command is being enforced at such a seemingly safe distance. Surprise is good. Life is full of it. And in training, whatever surprises us makes us stronger. Just keep taking him places and setting him up until there is no doubt that, whenever, wherever he's out and about, "here" means "Drop everything and come" no matter how far away he is.

Part Two: Tension Relief!

Once you have a dog who is coming reliably on a flexi (or long line) no matter the distraction, congratulations are in order—you've done a lot of hard work. However (ah, you just knew there was going to be a "however"!), what do you suppose will happen when you remove the leash? (Hint: The flexi produces a tension between the collar and the case you're holding, and that tension on his neck will disappear.) You guessed it: He probably won't come. Without the tension, he assumes that this time he is off leash for real; so he will naturally proceed to test the strictness of all the work you've just put into him. Because he needs to obey without leash tension, you must next rework your "here" command with the flexi locked out. Here's how:

- Pull your flexi line all the way out. Lock it (by pushing in the brake and the locking button*) and lay the case down on the floor. Let your dog frolic and be distracted. Then call him: "Here." If he comes, praise and release. Continue practicing in different locations with different distractions until he finally chooses to test your resolve. This forced error is essential if he is to learn that you can still correct him when he's off leash—that's the key concept here!

- When he doesn't come, make for the nearest section of the flexi line. Your dog may be off to your left, but if the closest piece of line is to your right, go thataway.

- Saying nothing, just step on the line and, tightrope-style, walk on it until you arrive at a dog—specifically, the dog who didn't come when you called.

- Slowly reach for his collar, and, briskly backing up the whole way, lead (drag, if necessary) your dog to where you were when you called him. With every few backward steps say, "Here." Yes, you're repeating a command (usually a no-no), but you're also enforcing it each time, which makes it okay. Don't forget to praise and release when he gets to you.

After a while, one of two things will happen.

First possibility: Your dog will start coming when you call him because he doesn't enjoy being dragged by the collar. Congratulations! Continue practicing, varying your locations and other distractions. When your dog is consistent no matter what is going on around him, you're ready to move on to the light line.

Second possibility, and the more common, alas: Your dog will try to escape. Seeing you approach, he says, "See ya later!" and bolts in the other direction. If you train in a large but ultimately enclosed area, it's no problem: He won't get far.

---

*The flexi model you have may differ. Read the accompanying instructions regarding the locking method for your particular model.

The key to working out this kink is composure: calm when walking the dog down, slow but deliberate in reaching for the collar, and casually decisive in walking him back to the starting point. The message: "You can run but you can't hide; I will always be able to get to you, so why not make this easy on both of us and come when I call?" Your dog's type will bear on how readily this message is sent and received.

Shy/Sensitive: When you walk the tightrope toward a shy/sensitive dog, it helps if you avoid making eye contact. Look at the ground as you slowly approach, and don't reach for the collar too abruptly. Walk briskly backward to the "call spot," where the praise and reward should be lavish.

Dominant: If your dog is not the sort to care whether you are walking him down or frog-marching him back to the call spot, you may need a higher level of correction. You can start with a few collar tugs as you are backing up with him. Remember to praise and reward when you arrive at the call spot. (Corrections are not punishment and must always be delivered with patience and balanced with reward!)

Eventually your dog will realize that when you call him, he can either come to you or have you come get him. After a few "walk-downs" most dogs recognize the superior choice.

Once he is making the right choice reliably, run him through a round of appropriate distractions, individually and in multiples, over many weeks (or months!) of sessions to deepen his understanding before proceeding to the light line, the last proofing step before he learns to come off leash.

But for Those Dogs Who Have Been Walked Down Yet Persist in Defying Your Orders . . .

Unfortunately, this problem more than likely indicates that the basic steps haven't been taught well enough. Here's a diagnostic: Go back to a six-foot leash and call your dog. Does he come on the leash without distractions? Good. Now change location and add one more distraction. Does he still come? Great! Now try him with the flexi, first with and then without tension. Add distractions. Rerunning the drill at high speed is a reliable way of identifying the weak links. Once identified, they can be strengthened by remedial training. Nine out of ten times during the training of all commands, my students find they have to go back and retrain a previous step. The reasons, oh-so-numerous, include:

Rushing: "Hey, I went to step 2 and the dog came to me five whole times when I called. On to step 3!"

Denial: "Pookie is so smart, he already knows how to come on a leash. I'll go straight to the off-leash part of the program.

Breaks in Training: "Let's see, I think we were at step 9 in January (last training session), so I guess we pick it up with step 10" (even though it's July!!).

Inappropriate Levels of Correction: "Sweetums doesn't like it when Mommie tugs the leash, does he?" If you are unwilling to give the dog a correction he needs, you are nagging him, not training him. "Sweetums, why do you hide every time I pick up the leash?" Overly harsh corrections, on the other hand, result in fearful behavior.

Dog Life Changes: Adolescence can hit hard. One day the dog is saying, "What can I do for you?"; the next, he's saying, "What can I do *to* you?" Actually, if anything he's probably wondering what you can do for him. Keep track of whom you have at the end of your leash, and be flexible enough to adjust.

HANGING BY A THREAD

Before your dog can come reliably off lead, you must proof him on the next closest thing: the light line. This will seem to your dog like no line at all, until a correction is called for. The aim of this equipment change is to simulate being off lead and to make your dog think that, even when he feels free as a bird, that old bite can still get him. If he comes to that view, he will accept that the rules apply whether he is on leash or not. At that moment your work is done.

The light line should be used in a fenced area because it is light and has a tiny bolt. If a dog was running full blast and you stepped on the line, the little bolt would pop off and you would have a free dog. A dog that is still racing after squirrels after you call "here" is clearly not ready for the light line.

And if he's not ready?

If you have a dog who comes on leash, but persists in refusing to come off leash no matter how often you rerun the training, if your dog can somehow always detect the lightest light line, you may want to look into electronic collars. Did I hear a gasp? Now, calm down: An electronic collar is *not* the electric chair. I would never suggest anything that would cause your dog real pain. The zap from most electronic collars feels more like a tingle or vibration. Some offer a more uncomfortable level of output, but I've never found one that could remotely approximate being struck by a car. Innotek makes a nice seven-level model that accommodates most dogs. If seven levels is ineffective because your dog has the physical sensitivity of a rhino, then Dogtra or EDT collars are the next step. Can they be abused? Of course, but so can a six-foot leash if you're too quick and rough about tugging.

Long, long ago, in a galaxy far, far away, I was doing my little beginner classes at the animal shelter. Whenever someone had a dog who would come on leash but not off, my prescription after reviewing the steps with them was always to keep practicing. Having no children yet, I used to imagine that everyone could work two or three half-hour dog training sessions into the day. As I've since learned, some can, but most can't. But that doesn't change the absolute imperative of teaching your dog to come off leash. Sometimes a dog has lived off leash for too long; he naturally takes the freedom trail when the leash is removed, and that will to freedom can be immense. If that's your dog, and only you can judge, if seemingly endless repetitions are not doing the trick and you find yourself spending all your waking hours at the other end of a flexi, consider the collar. I know, the collars come with training videos, but some things can't be taught by video. *Always consult a qualified professional before using an electronic collar.* This is not a cop-out but a practical necessity. Coming off leash is simply not a skill your dog should live without. Speaking of practical necessity . . .

IN CASE OF EMERGENCY, BREAK DOG CLASS RULES!

It's the middle of the day, and the doorbell rings. Before you can get to the door, your three-year-old opens it, and your dog (still midlearning curve) heads for the hills (or whatever topographical feature seems most enticing). Worst-case scenario: the two-way street. This is the time to break all the rules you've learned so far! Call "here" to him as many times as you can; try yelling, "Who wants to go for a ride?" or the even more irresistible "Who wants to eat? Who wants a cookie?" Under such conditions, anything you can do that might return your dog to safety is fair game.

The *only* thing you shouldn't do is to run "at" your dog. Most likely, he will take this to mean you're initiating a game of chase, or else that you're threatening him; either impression will only make him run faster. If you can get your dog's attention, running away from him may well initiate a game in the other direction, with your dog chasing you. Opening a car door is helpful, as is squatting down and pretending you've just found something fascinating on the lawn. Again, such suggestions imply that your dog is looking at you.

When you've finally corralled your dog, DON'T yell or correct him in any way. You don't want him to conclude, "Okay, next time I'll be sure NOT to come back, because this is the thanks I get!" Grin and bear it (I feel your pain, believe me) and praise him lavishly. Bring him back into the house, attach the light line, and try to reset the same situation again, this time correcting his error. Postponing your nervous breakdown just long enough to do this will vastly benefit the cause of training and ultimately your mental health.

TEACHING "LET'S GO"

The Dog Who Wouldn't Walk

In Florida I met a Pekingese named Puffy. At four years old, Puffy still refused to walk on a leash. My first question for the owner was not my usual diagnostic ("Describe the symptoms of the problem" or "What do you think could be causing this behavior?"). My first question was "After four years of carrying this dog outside for everything from car trips to the call of nature, what made you decide that you'd had enough?!" Well, it seems Puffy had gotten a bit "puffier," so to speak. Only lately, facing a hernia, had the owner decided her behavior was totally unacceptable.

Puffy was carried to her first class in the prescribed condition—hungry, lonely, and/or bored, wearing a pink rhinestone-encrusted harness. And, boy, did she look bored! Her owner put her on the leash that she'd let Puffy drag around the house during the previous week in an attempt to introduce her to this foreign object. Defying even my own generous tolerance for the cheerful cutes, the owner would call, "Puffster, let's go!" The Puffster did nothing. The owner then whipped out a dog treat (at which point I'm noticing, "This dog looks like she just came from an all-you-can-eat night at the Olive Garden. Will she work for food?!"). If the Puffster even noticed the treat, she didn't let on. I suggested that the owner take a step or two away, without looking back at the dog, but continuing her cheery encouragements. Now, in addition to the owner's dulcet tones, there was the even lovelier sound of the Puffster's rear puff being dragged on the ground, looking a little as if she were being towed on a boogie board. Amazingly, she showed no sign of discomfort. In a voice now full of wheezy despair, the owner allowed that this unlikely tableau had been the norm from the first time she tried to take the Puffster, as a puppy, for a walk.

I suggested that Puffy slip into something less comfortable, for dragging at least: lose the harness and change into a buckle collar (Dog Trainer's Little-known Fact #78: 99.9 percent of all the dogs who pull on their leashes or who won't walk are wearing harnesses). Harnesses are fine for sled dogs: Pulling is their business! But any dog not carrying you across the tundra needs to wear a buckle collar. Unfortunately, Puffy, a typical diva—you would be, too, if carried everywhere since birth—didn't appreciate the wardrobe change. She reared up in protest and then flopped on her back. Her owner continued walking and talking in a cheery voice. Puffy continued to be dragged, now on her back. She appeared to be enjoying the cloud formations. Seeing the owner come to the end of her aerobic capacity, I decided this had to stop. I suggested that we change the terrain. Instead of pulling Puffy over grass, I proposed to pull her on the pavement, expecting the discomfort would bring her to her feet if not her senses. But the stone-cold Puffster was not fazed. We then got the hose and soaked the driveway, hoping she would demonstrate an aversion to getting wet. Not the Puffinator! That's when I decided the gloves had to come off. It was then that I suggested that we go to a new training location.

Down by the not-in-use-since-the-1960s railroad tracks I laid out my plan. (Don't worry: I'm not a cartoon villain—we didn't tie the poor Puffster to the tracks.) The owner was to give Puffy the command "Let's go" and walk ten paces. The trick was that they would be walking down the middle of the railroad tracks where every so often there would be a large bump for Puffy to contend with. We had a one-hour lesson scheduled, but I was betting that Puffy would get the hang of walking in about half that time. On the first attempt, Puffy flopped on the tracks and was dragged on her belly the entire ten paces, bumping over the ties. On the second attempt she switched to her back. On the third attempt she stayed upright but dragged with a force that would shame a mule. That's when I introduced Puffy to the charms of a prong collar. I had briefed the owner on the mechanics of a prong (see page 40 for more details) and the once-reluctant but now-desperate mistress practically "Riverdanced" with anticipation as she saw me put it on Puffy's neck. Puffy immediately did a belly flop, followed by something resembling the "stop, drop, and roll" you learn in grammar school, followed by a standing-mule drag, followed by . . . walking! And more walking. Then another weak attempt at a drag, followed immediately by . . . more walking. It would not be an exaggeration to say that the sun came out, the birds started singing, and Puffy's owner looked twenty years younger! Okay, that would be a slight exaggeration, but you get the idea. From that point on, the woman's life was transformed by the fact that Puffy was a champion walker, and although every once in a blue moon the Puffster would be back to her old tricks, those spells were short-lived as long as she had on her new collar. Roll credits.

FINALLY, HOW TO TEACH "LET'S GO"

The perfect "Let's go" command results in dog and handler looking as if they are walking as one. The dog remains at the handler's side, not forging ahead and not lagging behind. The dog's head is up, not sniffing the ground, but paying close peripheral attention for any change of speed or direction by his owner. When the owner comes to a stop, the dog sits, attentively waiting for the next command.

Here's a test: Hold both arms out in front of you. Is one longer than the other? Are there scrapes on the knuckles of the longer one caused by dragging it when you walk? Unless you've needed an extra long sleeve since childhood, I'm guessing your condition is not congenital: Your dog is a "puller" or a "lagger." As you can probably infer, a puller pulls you and a lagger makes you pull him, but the results are the same. You've come to the right page.

"Let's Go" vs. "Heel"

I find the most mild-mannered people, when asked to command their dogs to heel, instantly develop Gestapo characteristics. I don't know the psychological reasons, but the symptoms are unmistakable. Their voices drop two octaves, they stand rigidly and bark rather than speak the order. Naturally, the effect is not the one desired but, more typically, that of a dog cowering in fear as she tries to figure out this mad authoritarianism, then crumbling into confused disobedience as the command is barked in ever louder frustration, finally to be tuned out. "Heel," like "come" (remember "here" vs. "come"?), has been lost to bad-training associations. For this reason, I use the more pleasant and distinctive "Let's go." If you must use "heel," however, be sure to subdue your inner *Kommandant* first.

The Checklist

Dog: hungry, lonely, and/or bored. Motivator: You know what works. Reconnaissance: distraction free. And we're off . . .

Phase One: The Lure

Note: If you are teaching a puppy, I'm assuming you've already accustomed him to the leash and collar by following the exercises in chapter 4. If not, go back and do so before proceeding!

- Take your motivator (we're going to use food in this example) and let your dog know you have it. (Having a little déjà vu here?)
- With the dog sitting or standing to your left, take the leash in your left hand. I prefer a four-footer; you can use any length you want, but a longer one will seem cumbersome, at least initially. You want just a bit of slack—too much and the dog will pull ahead, too little and he'll be up walking on his hind legs! Now—very important!— keep your left hand on your left hip, in line with the seam of your pants. If your hand begins to slip, the dog will have more latitude, and you know what he'll do with that. I don't care how you keep your hand fastened to your side—thumb hooked in belt works, but if you can

do it with Krazy Glue or Velcro, be my guest. Just don't move your arm.

- Try to hold the lure in your left hand, too. For those with small hands or long leashes, you may use the right hand, BUT you must bring it over to your left side! This means a bit of upper-body contortion, but otherwise the dog will be cutting in front of you trying to get the food.

Right brain/left brain: I can hear some of you saying, "I'm a rightie, so this is awkward. Can't I do this on my right side?" Absolutely! I'm a rightie myself, but because AKC Obedience rules dictate that the dog be on the left for competition heeling and that's where I started in dog training, I'm a left side "lifer"!

- Looking at your dog, say his name, following with the command "Let's go," and start walking. Sounds simple? *I can't begin to tell you how many people have a problem doing this. They say "Let's go" and then don't move. They wait for the dog. So the dog stands or sits there waiting for them. In teaching, as in young love, if you want something, you've gotta make the first move!*
- Keep your hands in their correct positions, and alert the dog if he strays from his own—if he tries to lag, tell him, "Hurry," and continue moving. If he tries to forge ahead, say, "Easy." All the while, you should praise him when he is just where he should be. Any variations out of correct position will be minimal because of the small amount of leash you've given him.
- Heeling is a relatively fast behavior to program, because the dog is getting a lot of real-time feedback, hearing at every moment whether he is right or wrong. It will sound like endless jabber: "Let's go, good boy. Ah-ah, easy. Yes! Good boy, excellent. Ah-ah, hurry. Good, good boy." But it does work. You should be looking at your

dog and making continual eye contact to amplify the communications. After a *few* successful steps, release with "Okay" and give your dog the treat.

- Start again, this time increasing the number of steps.
- After you've increased your steps a few times, try to walk your dog in a circle. Keeping the leash fairly slightly taut, walk him in a counterclockwise circle first. Being on the inside of the circle will be easier for him because he won't have to move as fast.
- When he masters the counterclockwise circle, try him with the reverse (turning toward your right, with the dog on the outside of the path). This action may bring the first sign of resistance, as a dog who is maybe already ambivalent about walking nicely on lead realizes that his job just got a bit harder! Encourage, praise, and flash the motivator, coaxing your dog to keep up with you. Remember, proper leash tension minimizes room for resistance and error.

Phase Two: Random Rewards

After a week of rewarding with food or toys every time, you'll begin to wean your dog off the lure, offering a reward unpredictably and with less frequency. Start by furnishing a treat (food or toy or play) every other time. In the next round, give it up on the first, then the fifth, the sixteenth, etc., until he's down to only two rewards for each session: one for his first perfect "Let's go" and one for the last. Little does the poor dog realize that he is gradually being nudged off the chuck wagon! As usual, eventually, your love and praise will be sufficient rewards.

Of course, we don't discourage the occasional bonus: There will be times when your dog has done such an incredible job walking next to you (perhaps amid distractions over and above the call of duty), and in those cases you may give an unscheduled treat of *his* choice!

Phase Three: On the Road Again

For those of you whose dogs are cruising through this, congratulations! But you know by now progress means moving from easier to harder, not the other way around. Change venue, and then proceed to work with other distraction factors in your private repertoire. You must work up to the most distracting situations you can imagine. Remember, you could be walking the dog virtually anywhere, and there is a convenient place for him to race ahead or lag behind—both are a drag. Think parks, soccer games, mall parking lots, wooded trails, city sidewalks, mosh pits—*anywhere* that will test your dog's idea of what the "Let's go" command really means.

Once you've accomplished that goal, you can move on smartly over to "Getting Loose and Letting Go" (page 170).

Isn't this easy? It's not? Okay, listen: Every dog has his own strengths and weaknesses. Remember the kid who was great in math but lousy in English? My all-time heeling champ was a lousy sit-wait dog. Sometimes what makes us good at one thing can actually be a disadvantage in other endeavors. Count your blessings (there's always a worse-behaved dog than yours!), and take the challenges as a natural part of life—on two legs or four!

But you didn't buy this book for life lessons. What can you do when your dog won't walk the walk?

COPING WITH A GOOD WALK SPOILED

Not every dog immediately takes to a controlled walk. Like the down, it's a very submissive behavior, and your dog may still have issues with your being leader of the pack. Or perhaps he still believes that he has choices: You want to get home ASAP before the rain turns from a drizzle into a deluge, while your dog thinks this is crackerjack weather to inspect all the neighbors' lawns—different species, different agendas. Take pity on him for his delusions. He will get over them ultimately: You're the one who has the food; you're the one who calls the shots! Meanwhile, here's a map to some of the most common roadblocks on the way to the perfect "Let's go":

The Incredible Edible Leash

One of the most common complaints I hear is that the dog bites on the leash when walking. Some resourceful canines work this stunt so well that they are able to walk the owners! Initially, there's something inexplicably cute about a dog prancing like a show pony, with his leash in his mouth, but the novelty is short-lived. Biters come to me either with leashes chewed beyond recognition, or else they wear the chain-link variety, inspired by the not unreasonable "Oh, yeah, chew this!" frame of mind. Eventually, however, this latter choice has you pulling his chain, giving you the hands of a dockworker. I know the tiny handle is leather, but no one has ever been able to walk a dog on a chain leash without having to resort to pulling on the chain itself. Furthermore, the retractables don't come in chain link—thank goodness!

I'd Like to Solve the Puzzle, Please

Two words: bad taste! Buy one of the bitter-tasting products described on page 42 and spray the leash with it right before leaving the house (better to do it before attaching the leash to the dog's collar!). Some dogs may require more profound bitterness to be put off, and that means soaking the leash overnight. (So know your dog before you buy the itty-bitty three-ounce spray!) If your dog considers the bitter spray to be a condiment, you may need something stronger. Peppermint breath spray, cinnamon breath spray, Tabasco sauce. Anything that will make the dog think "Yuck!" without killing him is fair game. And bring a bottle of whatever you use with you to refresh the "bite" (alcohol-based products tend to wear off quickly, as the alcohol evaporates). Be very careful to avoid the dog's eyes when you reapply.

The Champion Puller

If your dog could outpull a Siberian husky, or if he happens to *be* a Siberian husky or another type of sled dog with delusions of grandeur, you may want to try the following:

Turbo-charge the treat: You don't have to increase the frequency of reward, but you can upgrade to something he'd give his canines to have.

Collar change: If your dog is wearing a harness, now might be a good moment to kick yourself for skimming over chapter 3. Harnesses *are* for pulling! Switch to a buckle collar.

Head fake: Instead of walking in a predictable pattern (straight line, circle), make abrupt changes in your path. Take five steps forward and suddenly cut off to the right. Your dog, being on a short lead, will compensate for your erratic behavior with heightened alertness and responsiveness. This diverts his concentration from pulling.

Lagging, Dragging

Three Words: Remember the Puffster!

After failing to reform with food and toys, sometimes the only recourse is a collar change. And a terrain change. Did someone say "wet grass"? Go back and reread the Puffster railroad adventure for inspiration. Don't look at me that way: I'm not asking you to spay her without anesthesia. Little adjustments can tip the struggle in your favor. Need I repeat the mantra of hungry, lonely, and/or bored at this stage of your enlightenment?

The Searchers

Unless you search professionally for missing people, the dog who follows his nose never lifting it above the terrain is a problem.

Collar change: A possible fix for your inveterate bloodhound.

Back it up: If your searcher refuses to walk next to you, start by teaching him to walk *to* you. Stand in front of

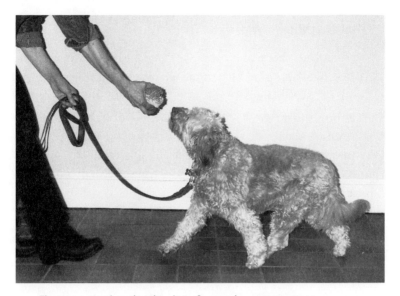

Figure 31. Luring the dog into forward movement.

him, with his favorite toy or food in your right hand, held centered ahead of you at a height appropriate to his height (belt-buckle high for a retriever, knee-high for a grasshopper, or at least a papillon). Holding the leash with your left hand, also centered, take a few steps back (figure 31). The dog should be looking up at the motivator, so adjust the height accordingly. After one or two steps in the right direction, release him with "Okay" and give him the reward, making sure that he must reach up for it (otherwise you'll be reinforcing his tendency to keep his head down). After you've increased to fifteen or twenty steps, it's time for you to start pivoting in and out of position. Here's what you do: Back up a few steps in the manner described above, then pivot so that the dog is on your left and you are now both facing forward in the same direction (the direction he was moving in). You'll also need to reposition the motivator from just ahead of you to alongside your left hip. Take one or two steps in this position, then pivot back in front for another step before the release. Eventually, you should be spending more time with your dog on the left than in front of you.

He's Looking at You, Kid!

Inevitably, there are people in my class who complain, "My dog won't stop looking at me when we walk. He's driving me crazy!" My immediate reaction is: "I'll take him!" It's not merely that I'm a sucker for attention. In fact, one of the hardest things to teach dogs in "competitive" obedience is how to walk in heel position without breaking eye contact. To quote the diva of domesticity, "It's a good thing." But if you can't handle the continuous eye lock, it will eventually stop without encouragement—that's how hard it is for the dog to keep it up. Bring your chronic eyeballer to a dog club that offers competition-geared classes if you want to know how good you have it.

A Funny Thing Happened on the Way to . . .

Let's get one thing straight: You have been letting the dog take care of business before training "Let's go," correct? "Oh sure, yeah, of course . . . hmm." The reason I ask: *Some* owners (not your kind, of course) don't implicitly understand that controlled walking is not appropriate for "taking the dog for a walk" in the sense of bodily function. If a dog has to poop or pee, of course that will take precedence over walking nicely for you. Sorry, there are limits. When released with an "Okay," your dog has a right to sniff and potty freely. But I haven't gone completely wobbly on you: Even then, pulling won't be tolerated—a pop to the wise should be sufficient.

A dog who's been given the opportunity to relieve himself and still stops to mark every tree, pole, and person that you pass is a dog who needs correction: a tug on the collar plus an "ah-ah" administered with each infraction should break this habit.

Get a Jump on This

So your dog tried pulling and you've scotched that behavior. Then he tried lagging and dragging, and you nipped that in the bud, too. For many the obvious next anti-heeling maneuver will be to jump on you. There's the "kangaroo hop" in which the dog jumps on and off, on and off with every step that you take. There's the "guerrilla warfare tactic" of jumping up and then immediately off, before continuing to play along with your walking idea until a few steps later, when—Bam!—he jumps you again. And finally there's the "Velcro": The dog jumps up and hangs on for dear life, making it impossible to walk at all. If you're sure that your dog's genetic lines do not contain kangaroo, try these suggestions:

Collar change: Enough said.

Length of leash: Are you cutting him too much slack? If he's jumping up on you, then the answer's a definite "Probably!" A sufficiently taut rein doesn't allow enough give for your dog to jump up. If you start out with a tight leash, but find yourself absentmindedly slacking off, mark the point on the leash where your hand should be with a piece of electrical tape.

What goes up must come down, mustn't it?: Sure, except when humans surrender to the natural urge of pulling down on a dog who has jumped up. To the dog, this homo-canine wrestling may seem like a fabulous game. Better to teach your dog that he should *never* jump on anyone. (I bet he doesn't jump only on you or only during walks—am I psychic?) Skip to chapter 6, where I elaborate on techniques for the common problem of jumping in the company of strangers. Apply them, and your dances with kangaroos will be a thing of the past.

Dogs Who Love Chasing Cars and the Cars That Hit Them

Actually, for some dogs, the things to chase could be cars, bicycles, joggers, or running animals—no moving object too big or too small. But when the object has a fender, chasing behavior is at its most dangerous for all parties involved—for the driver who swerves to avoid your dog; for your dog who may get hit by the car anyway; for the jogger crossing nearby; and on and on. Many times, a high prey drive is the root of this problem. Prey drive is the dog's hardwired urge to chase moving objects. Retrievers were bred to run after a bird shot down;

Border collies, to herd sheep in the field; fox terriers, to bolt a fox from its lair. Believe it or not, the dog sleeping on your couch retains most of his ancestral drives—and those of you who have high–prey drive dogs know it! One minute you're walking your dog; the next minute you're a charm dangling from the end of a leash with a guided missile pulling on the other end.

Collar change: If you ever had the slightest doubt about prong collars, hyper-prey drive will make a believer of you.

Early warning system: You can't buy one; you can only cultivate one. Your dog telegraphs his intentions long before he acts. Your job is to correct him when you see him *thinking* about a lunge, and since you're attentively watching him while you walk, you'd certainly notice the signs: He stares at a moving object. He may start moving slowly in its direction, possibly in a skulking crouch. A simple verbal warning ("ah-ah") may be enough to dispel the wicked thoughts from his head. If it doesn't, follow immediately with a tug on the leash. If he responds by looking away from his potential quarry, praise him and continue walking. If his mobilization continues or escalates, order up a sit-wait. Walk a few steps and sit-wait again. Message: He's allowed to walk when he behaves, and when he doesn't, he'll be doing a lot of sitting and waiting!

To Have and to Hold: Infringement of Leash-Ownership Rights

Some dogs want to hold the leash in their mouths, others just want to put a paw on it to control the walk. Some dogs put one paw on the leash (going for the limp-along-Lassie effect), and there are those who use two, as if to say, "We're both civilized adults. Can't we work something out here?" Either way, if your dog engages in this kind of behavior, he is obviously in violation of your property rights (as the owner of both him and the leash), to say nothing of your walk-leading prerogative as his provider. Maybe your neighbors think these theatrics are entertaining, but I have to insist that your dog walk on all fours like—you should pardon the expression—a dog!

The Sweet Spot

The laws of physics tell us that there is a theoretical point on the back of your dog's neck where a leash may be attached to his collar and be out of his reach from either side. That's the spot over which to hold the leash so that she keeps her paws to herself. This may not prevent her rebellion by other means, but we can only deal with one tactic at a time.

Hannibal Lecter

If you've ever observed your dog aggressively lunge at people, animals, cars, etc., it's time to call in a professional. There's a huge difference between a dog who gives chase because of a heightened prey drive and a dog chasing something with malicious intent to do serious damage. Many times, the difference is not obvious enough for the dog owner to detect. Call your local dog club and ask if they can recommend a trainer who has experience in this kind of problem. As always, you want first to observe this person teaching someone else's dog—preferably one with similar problems. Don't wait: the longer the aggression goes on, the harder it is to fix!

Lions and Tigers and Bears, Oh My!

The polar opposite of the high–prey drive pack? The meek and worried dogs. In their own way, they, too, can bring a fine walk to a halt. Some dogs are innately meek and worried. In other cases, however, dogs have become this way because the owners have unwittingly created this personality. For example, if there's a loud noise while we're on our walk and the dog cowers, I would say in a cheerful voice, "You silly puppy, you're fine," and keep walking. Compare this with the more common "Oh, my poor snookums baby, let Mommie pick you up and here's a cookie" method, which tends to confirm that something extraordinarily frightening just happened and then rewards the fearful response to it. BEWARE rewarding fearful behavior! If you pretend you don't notice and then take the Mary Poppins road of chipper but not coddling reassurance, your walk can continue without incident or negative programming. In time you may find that your dog is actually not so fearful by nature, but rather learned to be as a way of gaining reward, in attention or treats. Be sure to reward him with praise when there is a scary noise and he remains calm!

Of course, the truly meek may never inherit the earth because of their aversion to walking anywhere but in their own house and yard. Remember Winnie-the-Pooh's friend Piglet? He spends most of every story saying, "Oh, dear," and wringing his hands. This is what the meek and worried dog would say, if he could. Such a dog needs extra motivation in the form of higher-quality treats (deli-sliced turkey instead of cheese, for example), a slower-paced walk, and much more encouragement and praise ("Atta-boy, you can do it"). While taking care not to reward the undesirable behavior, you should give the rewards much more frequently and keep the walk much shorter than that for the average dog. For the super-timid, two steps, a treat, and back to base camp is acceptable. If you add a few steps every couple of days, you'll get your own reward eventually: One day the dog will just jump-start and keep walking. Nevertheless, the meek type of dog always requires tremendous patience. So don't start a training session unless you're in a great mood to begin with!

Caveat, owner: There are always a few Puffsters out there passing themselves off as meek. Differentiating timidity and willful passivity can be tricky. My suggestion is to presume the former initially, but if you're getting nowhere fast consult a professional trainer for a second opinion on your dog's temperament.

GETTING LOOSE AND LETTING GO: SOME NEW MOVES

No, I am not plagiarizing some training manual from the Age of Aquarius. Trippy though the heading may sound, the point here is simply to bring your dog, now thoroughly trained on the "Let's go" command, to the next level: Teaching him to sit when you stop and to execute his turns with grace. His "Let's go" need not be perfect (yet!), but his pulling, sniffing, lagging, and lunging days should be behind him, and he should be adept at staying in heel position. Okay, let the sunshine in.

I STOP, THEREFORE YOU SIT

Teaching a dog to sit when you stop walking is fairly simple. "Finally, something simple!" However ("Uh-oh . . ."), your dog must be in heel position or else the sit will be crooked, wide (he's too far away for you to control), lagged (you're pulling him), or forged (he's pulling you).

Teaching the Sit—Part One

- It is imperative to start with your dog in heel position: He is sitting on your left, facing the same direction as you are, and his shoulder is aligned with the seam of your pants.
- At this point, you're still holding the leash somewhat taut, not in a straight line, but forming a J (figure 32).

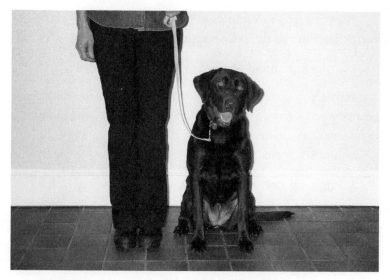

Figure 32. Leash somewhat taut but forming a J.

In any case, it's not loose and it's in your left hand—righties just have to deal with it.

- You have a motivator (food, toy) on hand, but not visible.
- Begin moving forward. When you halt, bringing both feet together, your right foot's final step should be half a normal step and your left foot's final step should be at half speed as it comes up to meet your right foot. I know, I was no *Soul Train* dancer myself, but it's not as difficult as it sounds! The reason for this fancy footwork is that if your walking comes to a more abrupt stop, your dog won't notice until it's too late and he's way past heel position. This is no reflection on your dog's intelligence. Even a human co-walker trying to keep pace next to you would keep going if you stopped abruptly. But when the human does it, he's only human; when the dog does it we cry "sloppy training!" That's a dog's life for you.
- After your controlled halt, say, "Sit," at the same time gently pulling **straight up** on the leash. Notice the bold italics. If I had my way, these words would be on a page of their own, such is their importance! More on that later.
- Evaluate the sit, release, reward, and praise your dog.

Sit Happens

Here are a few examples of incorrect post-ambulatory sits and what you can do to fix them:

My dog sat ahead of me (forged sit).

Either you gave him too much leash as you were heeling or you stopped abruptly and then sat your dog rather than doing both simultaneously. Tighten up on the leash and be sure to tell him to sit *as you are making him sit by pulling straight up.*

My dog sat behind me and is staring up at my butt (lagged sit).

Especially embarrassing if it's the same expression as when he's staring at your face—let's fix this immediately! You either gave him too much leash, so he was already south of heel position when you gave the "sit" command, or you let your arm swing backward as you tugged on the leash, causing him to rock back into his sit. Solution: For the sit to occur in the proper position, your dog must be walking in the proper relation to you. Keep the lead taut during the sit so no rockbacks can occur.

He's not facing the same way I am— he's looking across me.

No matter how quick on the pull-up you may be, some dogs will find a way to throw their rear way out to the left. Most such dogs have extremely long bodies. Not just dachshunds and basset hounds—any breed (or nonbreed, for that matter) can have a long body. A dog who is as long as he is tall is referred to as "square." He looks like a nicely proportioned box, if you will. It's easier for him to stay straight, as there isn't much body to get out of line. A long-bodied dog, on the other hand, must (1) realize that he *does* have a rear end and (2) work to keep it moving in the same trajectory as the front end. Easy to explain, not as easy for him to do. Technically, his front end is still in heel position, but his rear end is angled away from his owner's body (figure 33). To stop this, you're going to have to switch the leash to your right hand a few steps before you stop

Figure 33. Dog's front end is correct, but his rear is angled too far away from his owner's body.

Figure 34. Guiding dog's flank back in line.

moving. Your right hand will be reaching across your body
and resting on your left hip—a little contorted, I know, but at
least your left arm gets a break from pulling and is now
responsible for keeping your dog's rear end in line. So, as you
begin your "right foot short–left foot slow" dance, twist to the
left and if necessary guide the dog's outside left flank with
your hand in the direction of your left leg (figure 34).

If that's too Cirque du Soleil for your taste: Instead of bending and twisting, you can use a wall, a couch, or a narrow hallway to correct your dog's rear drift. Just walk along, with six
to twelve inches between your dog's left side and the wall or
other obstacle. You can start with a bit more breathing room if
your dog initially seems claustrophobic.

The Wrap and the Pendulum

Sometimes a dog will throw his rear end out of line as he
wraps his head around your left leg, trying to look at your
face or get ahead of you. Dogs with longer necks can accomplish this without moving their front end out of heel position.
To correct, make sure that your dog is truly in heel position. Next, I want you suddenly to develop an affliction that

causes your right arm to swing like a pendulum, close to and across your body. If you do this correctly and consistently until your dog's wrapping is cured, your dog won't think you're intentionally bumping into him. He will, however, notice that you've developed a twitch that will cut off excess dog if said dog is twisted up or has forged on ahead of you. IMPORTANT! Know your dog's physical and emotional sensitivity levels! Too harsh of a correction will shatter your dog's trust, and too light will possibly create a great game of Dodge-the-Arm.

Teaching the Sit—Part Two

After about a week, you and your dog should be halting and sitting like pros! Now it's time to drop the verbal "sit" command and have an automatic sit. To get there, start using the verbal "sit" every other time you halt. Initially, if your dog doesn't sit, gently tug up on the leash. If, after a day or so, he's still not sitting automatically when you halt, your gentle tug should become a corrective pop, just as you would administer for a refusal to obey the "sit" command. At this point you can safely assume that your dog is refusing to sit either because he is distracted or imagines he has a choice.

FOR A CHANGE OF PACE

Let's say you and "Droop-a-Long" are a half mile into your evening saunter and you realize that you mistakenly left your meat loaf in the oven. If ole Droops is a one-speed dog, I'm guessing that the firefighters will get to your house before you do. I can hear those of you with fast dogs chuckling at this point. Well, chuckle on! What happens when you and Flash are a block from home and you see Mrs. Nosy Neighbor knocking on your front door? You start dragging your feet and watching the grass grow, but how is this slowdown to work if Flash continues heading home at Warp 3, with the aim of greeting Mrs. Nosy Neighbor as if she's from Publishers Clear-

ing House? Such eventualities, from the awkward to the cata-
strophic, can be avoided by teaching change of pace.

Teaching the Slow Pace

- For this exercise you'll be walking in a small circle, eight
  to ten feet in diameter, with the dog in heel position on
  the INSIDE of the circle (i.e., a counterclockwise walk).
  As you know from NASCAR races, the inside-track cars
  don't need to go as fast to keep up. That's why people are
  always looking for the inside track. But you will take the
  outside track, working a little harder for the sake of your
  dog's learning.
- This time, the leash is relatively loose, but you want to be
  able to control your dog before he gets too far out of heel
  position. You'll use a reining motion rather than a tug to
  keep your dog in position.
- Say your dog's name and "Let's go," and begin walking at
  a normal pace, telling your dog, "Easy," if he starts to
  forge ahead. (In fact there shouldn't be enough slack for
  him to forge much at all.) After a few steps, slow down to
  half your usual pace, saying, "Easy," just before reducing
  speed. Maintain the slow and steady pace. Use the "easy"
  command and a little tension on the leash as needed to
  keep your dog in position. Remember to praise your dog
  as you walk and he keeps pace.
- Make sure to keep your feet on your "track." If your left
  foot runs into your dog's path, he (especially if he's a
  small breed) will attempt to forge or lag in order to avoid
  a collision.
- After a few slow paces, you will resume normal walking
  speed. To do this, tell your dog to hurry, take a quick
  short step with your right foot, give a motivational tug
  on the leash to get him (and you!) moving normally again.
  Praise exuberantly and release!
- Until your dog understands the change-of-pace concept
  (which usually takes about a week), don't end with a formal halt. Instead, release with an exuberant "Okay!",
  praise, and reward.

- When your dog has mastered change of pace in a circle, you can start practicing in a straight line.
- Mix it up: Vary the length of your slow walk—sometimes ask your dog to walk very slowly for twenty paces and then go back to a brisk normal pace, and sometimes do only two or three slow steps followed by a halt. Dogs love the challenge of this game, which has the wonderful by-product of teaching him to be more attentive to you!

Teaching the Fast Pace*

- As with the slow pace, you'll be walking counterclock-wise in a small circle, eight to ten feet in diameter, with the dog in heel position (you already know that this means on your left side).
- Your leash is not tight, but not loose, and you'll use a reining motion rather than a tug to keep your dog in position.
- Begin at a normal pace and tell your dog, "Easy," if he starts to forge ahead—he shouldn't be able to stray far given the right amount of leash. After a few steps, change to a quicker pace. Just before you begin to accelerate, tell your dog, "Hurry."
- Always use the leash to keep your dog in position and remember to praise as you're moving. Also, stay "on track," keeping your feet out of his way.
- After a few steps at a fast pace, slow back to your normal pace. Use your "easy" command a step or two before you slow down to normal, slowing less abruptly until he's more responsive to that command. Praise exuberantly and release! Repeat, going a few extra steps the next time, and the next, and so on.
- Until your dog understands change of pace, don't end

*The fast pace can be anything from a brisker walk to a flat-out sprint! The exact speed depends largely on the handler and the dog's comfort level. I encourage you to teach your dog the fastest pace that you can both manage COMFORTABLY. And if top speed happens to be a jog or run, teach a "slower fast pace" first, and work up from there. You may not always be up for a sprint when he is!

with a formal halt. Instead, release with an exuberant "Okay!", praise, and reward.

- When your dog can speed up in the circle, start training in a straight line.
- Vary the length of your fast-walk interval, just as you did with the slow.
- Don't forget to gradually fade out those rewards. You want (*need!*) your dog walking beside you because you told him to, *not* because you're holding a tennis ball or a dog treat.

ROAD APPLES

In a perfect world, all of you who have read up to this part would have dogs happily prancing beside you, changing pace with ease. Those of you with Stepford Dogs may skip ahead to the next section, entitled "You Turn."

For persistent lagging and dragging issues, reread (what else?) "The Champion Puller" (page 164) and "Lagging, Dragging" (page 164) for inspirations and solutions. If your dog is still having a hard time with change of pace, give him a week off from it. During that week, work on the regular controlled walking, making sure to clear up any power-struggle issues or confusions he may evince. Then go back and reteach change of pace. Any advanced-level behavior (such as change of pace) must be built on a rock-solid understanding of the fundamentals. One step back for two steps forward.

YOU TURN

To round out your dog's walking-on-leash education, you shall teach him how to change direction. The move is called an about turn and it goes like this:

- You are walking with your dog in a straight line.
- Tell your dog to hurry and slowly begin turning to your

right, making a U-turn. Pay attention to your left shoulder, and don't let it lag behind you or you will inadvertently increase the lead and decrease your guiding leash tension.

- When you have completed the turn and are now going in the opposite direction, bring your pace back down to normal pace.
- Praise, reward (randomly, of course!), and release.

I bet you read that section and said, "Hey! She has me telling the dog to *hurry* WHILE I'm supposed to turn *slowly*. What's up with that?" The reason for the seeming contradiction is that even though you're slowing down, the dog, who is now on the outside track of the turn, has to hustle to keep up with you, who are now on the inside for a change.

You can use food or a toy as a motivator to get your dog to hurry on the turn. Keep it in your right hand and out of sight. As you're about to begin your turn, move your hand so it's in front of the dog's nose (which would mean your right hand is by your left leg). Now he's interested! As you turn, the lure remains within inches of his nose until you're facing the opposite direction. Then release, praise, and surrender the treat, which you know by now will fade off into the sunset one day.

LOOSEN UP!

When you and your dog are a well-oiled, synchronized walking machine (no more lagging or pulling!), that's the time to ease your leash tension. How much? Up until this point, the steady, gentle pull has kept the clip of your leash straight up and down, but now you may add enough slack so that the bolt hangs straight down. With practice, he should be walking just the same without the continuous feed of corrective tension. If at any time your dog regresses, go back to reining. Try to catch the little digressions in your dog's position *before* his training unravels into lagging and pulling again!

OFF LEASH

With the elimination of tension, the part of the leash hanging under your dog's chin from the bolt looks like a necktie, and in fact it has become a nonfunctional accessory. So when does it become purely ornamental? Or, to put it another way, when is your dog going to be ready to walk off leash? When he no longer requires correction in walking at different paces AND has complete mastery of "here."

That's a theoretical state, which can be achieved for most practical purposes. But I'm a firm believer in keeping even your wunderdog on a leash while you walk. I'm not talking about his inalienable right to an untethered romp in a fenced-in area. I'm talking about walking on the sidewalk or on the road, where a leash can protect him from the unforeseen danger or freak-out. Dogs can be trained to do amazing things, but the dog who can absolutely never be lured into speeding traffic by the sight of a dashing squirrel—that dog is pure fantasy. He's only canine, as you are only human. Why bet his life on the unprovable alternative hypothesis?

CHAPTER 6

Rules of Canine Etiquette

Meet and Greet: The Dog Social Experience!

It is a truth universally acknowledged that a dog in possession of a perfect walk must be in want of some etiquette. Well, perhaps not, but he's got to have it anyway. Otherwise, we all live in anarchy.

If you've read to this point, I'm going to assume that you are a dog owner and, as such, have had occasion to take your dog for a walk. (Unless you've collected him from the breeder or shelter in the last twenty minutes, this is a bet I can't lose.) And if you've taken your dog for a walk, chances are you've encountered other dogs and their owners. Following custom, you've likely allowed your dog to "visit" with the other dogs while you and the owners chatted. If you were lucky, the encounter ended without incident and you and your dog headed home. Otherwise, you may have wound up at the veterinary clinic or even the hospital to be treated for a dog bite. How could this happen? Unfortunately, it's not so rare. Fortunately, by following some simple rules, you and your dog can greatly reduce the chances of becoming a statistic.

RULE #1—KEEP YOUR EYES ON YOUR DOG

This is a situation when it's okay to violate the manners we're taught as children, specifically the rule "Always look at someone while he or she is speaking to you." You should be watching your dog and the other dog he is meeting, alert to any signs of a potential altercation (see Rule #3). So should that lout you're talking to, but he probably doesn't have your advantages, such as that of having read this book.

RULE #2—NEVER PRESUME

Presumption is a faux pas in canine affairs no less than in human ones. Your dog has always been great with other dogs. This person says that her dog is "friendly"—better yet, he is a star in competitive obedience. Good for them. Watch out anyway. Just because your dog is generally sociable, don't assume there is anything like a canine golden rule; there isn't. I've seen obedience champs chomp at other dogs with nary a provocation in sight. You never know.

RULE #3—LEARN TO READ DOG BODY LANGUAGE

Of course dogs have body language, too! In fact, theirs is much more obvious and meaningful to them. Showing teeth is never a friendly smile; wagging one's tail with short stiff movements can signal aggression; and a dog walking slowly and stiffly toward another is not thinking good thoughts (geriatric dogs being a possible exception). Intent or at least contemplation of aggression may also be manifested by ears pulled back, a lowered head, or a tail wagging low. The signal variations could fill a book of their own. When in doubt, play it safe and stay back.

Corollary #1 to Rule #3: Growling is not talking, unless you count cussing. When you hear it, he needs a pop.

RULE #4—MIND YOUR DOG'S MANNERS

Don't let your dog go nose-to-nose or nose-to-any-other-part with another dog. I know: Tell a baby not to cry. That's why there's a leash, even on your walkmeister. What may seem to you like a friendly or amorous gesture on his part may be taken amiss by the other dog who reads it as aggression. Aggression may even be your dog's intent for all you know. Make him keep that nose to himself.

RULE #5—REMEMBER AUNT BERTHA

That old lady with the powdered face you hated to hug and kiss. Gross! Forced displays of affection are generally not enjoyed by either party. If your dog is reluctant to approach another whether out of shyness or real fear, your pushing him to make nice is asking for trouble. Perhaps the other dog gave yours an aggressive "back off" signal, which you, more attuned to human subtleties, failed to notice. If your dog's a wallflower, let him be: He knows his own kind better than you do.

RULE #6—DOGS ARE NOT LITTLE PEOPLE IN FUR COATS: PRELUDE TO A KISS

The biggest misunderstandings about dogs generally come from projecting human motivations on canine gestures that seem to correspond to something humans would do. A common error is to imagine when a dog is licking another dog's mouth that the two are "kissing." That makes the behavior comprehensible, even heartwarming to us. It's potentially a form of submission that could be friendly or fearful, and could very well end in a major dogfight for little Hotlips.

CHAPTER 7

Behavior Problems

Top Ten Behavior Problems Frequently Used as Temporary Insanity Pleas

With very little fanfare, let me list the top ten behavior problems that I get called upon to solve:

1. "My dog jumps [on me, my kids, the door, Uncle Clyde]."
2. "My dog barks."
3. "My dog digs."
4. "My dog chews things he shouldn't."
5. "My dog doesn't listen to me."
6. "My dog charges through doors."
7. "My dog begs at the table."
8. "My dog steals things [usually food] from counters and/or tables."
9. "My dog acts like a maniac when greeting me, my family, and anyone who comes through the door."
10. "My dog chews his leash while it's attached to his collar."

Quite a list!! Let's start at the top and work our way down.

PROBLEMS #1 AND #9: MY DOG JUMPS

(And acts like a maniac when greeting us or visitors!)

We hold these truths to be self-evident regarding dogs and the guests they jump on:

- that people whom you have invited to your house and who don't care for dogs will always show up dressed in white
- that on that day your dog will have spent his morning frolicking in the yard, rolling in "God-knows-what"
- that among this foulness will be earth, mulch, and waste of his own making
- that he will have been let back into the house, accidentally, by your five-year-old before your guest arrives, and at the exact moment . . .
    1. that you open the door, your guest will, upon seeing a filthy dog, let out a shriek, compelling the dog to investigate this fascinating utterance, which he can do properly only by means of a face-to-face meeting, and . . .
    2. that such guest, who has incited the meeting, cannot do otherwise than to throw up both her arms in a panic, unwittingly thereby making the gesture that, in dog language, is universally understood to mean "Jump on me!" and . . .

Your worst nightmare? Consider yourself lucky if you've been only dreaming it!

Let's first examine how a dog learns this abhorrent behavior. If you've had him since he was a pup, think back to those days when he was a little fluff ball, whose black button nose and adorable eyes you could barely stand to be away from. At that time, whenever you returned home, it was like a scene from an old movie about the man coming home from the war with his girl on the dock, and the music swelling at the climax of hugs and kisses. Let's face it—you loved those days. So as the days turned into weeks and months, there was a longing to preserve that magic of homecoming. Soon though, where passion would ordinarily fade, you notice it becoming more insistent and impatient: Once you had only to walk into the room and your eyes would meet, and he would run to you. "Once you have found him, never let him go, once you have . . ."

Lately, though, you notice he is barking as your car pulls into the garage. As a matter of fact, he's clawing at the door as you're turning the key. And the thrill of that ten-pound puppy jumping into your arms only yesterday (it seems) gives way to seventy pounds of canine muscle tackling your solar plexus. After that, who wouldn't feel resentful—maybe you even begin dreading the moment when you walk through the door? Perhaps you've even raised your voice, or worse, at him. Baby, where did our love go?

Your relationship will survive only if you try to see it from his perspective. The dog is deeply confused. From the first day you taught him it was okay to jump, you made him feel like the best little dog in the world for throwing himself at you. How's he supposed to know that you don't feel the same way now that he is sixty pounds heavier? Dogs have no body image, and your dog wouldn't dream of hurting you. His entire sense of right and wrong is a matter of pattern recognition. You may not have considered yourself a dog trainer before cracking this book, but unknowingly you did something that all dog trainers strive to do—it's called *shaping a behavior*. In other words, you rewarded the dog for jumping up, and now the dog does it perfectly!

The good news is that most things you teach aren't written in stone; what is shaped can be reshaped. But the success of the effort will absolutely depend on strict consistency (on the part of you *and* your family). Keeping the training up may seem an inconvenience or worse, unloving, at times, but in the long run you will reap the rewards of your dog's obedience—and avoid your guests' class-action suit.

For the Puppy Owners

First, let me address those of you who have a puppy or are thinking of getting one. Next to the command "here," "sit" is the second most important word to teach your puppy. Once learned, "sit" will become an integral part of his daily life. He will be told to sit before he eats, before he gets petted, before you attach his leash (to take him out), etc. It's a quid pro quo for lots of things he wants. And thus he will come to understand that before anything pleasant can occur he must sit first. You're on the right track when you notice that he sits before being told to—usually following a few months during which the "sit" command has been consistently used and enforced by all members of the family.

But until that moment, when puppy owners return home to their waiting dogs, I recommend the following:

1. Enter the house without saying a word.
2. Pick up the puppy's leash and go to the puppy (if you're following the rules, he's in a crate or barricaded in a small room; if you're not, you deserve whatever he's done to your property).
3. Still silent (ignore the jumping and fussing), put the leash on his buckle collar (you have been keeping his buckle collar on, right?), pick him up, and carry him outside to his designated "bathroom" area. If he's too big to carry, quickly walk him (on only a few inches of leash) outside and bring him to his designated spot.
4. Tell him to "go potty" or whatever command you've programmed. After he's finished (and you may need to repeat your potty command a few times), give him lots of praise and play with him.

The above procedure will pattern your dog to know that the "party" occurs not when you return (and you are both inside the house), but only after you have taken him outside.

This simple adjustment is critical and will make teaching the puppy how to greet your guests in a civilized manner (the "sit") much easier.

Help for Adult Dogs

Those with vaulting adult dogs, take heart! You can start by changing your homecoming ritual according to the program outlined for the puppies. Next, whenever someone is at the door, take the time to put a leash on your dog and use the "sit" command. If you know that you need two hands to answer the door—to sign for and receive a large package, for example—put the dog away so that at the very least he won't have the opportunity to demonstrate incorrect behavior. If the person at the door is coming in for a visit, instruct him or her to not look at or speak to the dog for at least twenty minutes. In the meantime the dog remains on the leash, and, depending on the level of his training, in a sit or a down position. At this point you pull out a very special toy for him—one that he loves but never gets except when there's company. I recommend something he can chew on, which gives him something to do other than stare at the guest. When the guest leaves, so does the toy (until the next visit). The purpose of the silent treatment is to make the guest's presence less of an incitement to riot. Earlier, guests were a source of entertainment—they squealed, they flailed, they made interesting noises when they hit the ground. And you—well, you were part of the act, too! Even though your reaction to your dog's conduct was negative (except for the time he took down your cousin Joe who was carrying a tray of those awful cupcakes your aunt Zelda made), the visitor's arrival was nevertheless exciting and interesting, to say the least. I highly recommend receiving a large group of guests, even if only for twenty minutes, just to let your dog practice the correct etiquette. Christmas dinner would not be the time to start experimenting, so do try to invent a less formal occasion. (Don't forget to include guest children—you want the dog to learn that he can't jump on anyone, no matter how small!) Look at it this way: You can't teach your four-year-old table manners if he never sits at the table to eat, right? The same applies for the dog. Set up the situation, and make sure it's one you can control while giving him a lot of attention.

After the twenty-minute silent treatment—during which you and your guest are certainly free to interact with each other—it is now permissible for the guest to greet the dog. As always, the correct greeting depends on his individual type (the dog's). If he's tightly wound, you can have the guest remain across the room and softly, without eye contact, greet the dog. The end. As the dog progresses in training, you can build up to petting and maybe even offering him a dog cookie, but go slow. A laid-back type, by contrast, would do well with eye contact and a more enthusiastic verbal greeting—perhaps even a quick pat on the head. The end. Again, as training progresses you can build on the interaction (and the number of guests), but the slow approach will prevent your dog from reverting to tackle mode. Let's rewrite the opening scene on page 185, having implemented the new rules:

1. Someone you have invited to your house, who doesn't care for dogs, shows up wearing white (new friend; the old ones never returned) and . . .
2. that day your dog was rolling in varieties of filth in your yard and . . .
3. was accidentally let back into the house by your five-year-old before your guest arrived, and at the exact moment that you . . .
4. open the door, your guest, seeing a filthy dog, lets out a shriek, prompting the dog to check out this intriguing soprano up close and personal but . . .
5. you give your dog a command to sit, which he does (*Yes!*) and then . . .
6. you take the leash you keep by the front door and attach it to his collar before . . .
7. you invite your (still wary) guest into the house and show her to the living room, but ask her nicely to

refrain from addressing the dog ("*No* problem!"), whereupon . . .

8. she notices that your dog, however unkempt, is lying next to you on the floor, on leash, chewing on something unrecognizable to her but really interesting to him and . . .

9. after twenty minutes you ask her to greet the dog in her most unenthusiastic voice (she complies yet again: a friend indeed!).

10. The dog calmly accepts the attention before returning full concentration to his toy.

Come again, please!

This could happen for you. But reprogramming your dog's greeting procedure won't happen without consistency (expect the same behavior every time—never reward the incorrect kind; always praise the correct action), plus commitment.

A Special Note for Those Visiting "Dog Experts"

There are a lot of self-professed "dog people" out there, but having good canine rapport is one of those skills that people tend to overstate. Their credentials may range from knowing someone who owns a dog to having had a dog when they were kids to owning a dog at the present time. But we know that even the latter does not an expert make. That fact, however, does nothing to stem the flow of unbidden and unwanted advice, which often as not may be utterly wrong for your type (or any type!) of dog. In addition to giving free advice, such people sometimes presume to take a free hand in administering a correction to your dog—the most classic being a knee to the chest! Besides doing physical harm, such a move can set your training back months if not years. (Knowing what you know now about the serious business of a physical correction, I hardly need explain the wherefores.)

Equally damaging to your training program can be the polite and well-meaning people who profess not to mind being jumped on. *They* may not mind, but your uncle Clyde does,

and jumpers tend not to keep records about personal preferences. Consisitency is essential.

You can deal with either kind of "dog people" one of two
ways: First, you can explain to them that you are training the
dog and that you are following a method that departs from
their obviously quite sound advice. (Tell 'em it's new, "Euro-
pean" or "ancient Japanese"—whatever it takes.) They may
think you've joined some crazy cult, but most will respect the
fact that it's your house and your dog, and leave you to your
weird benighted ways. Second, an option for dealing with the
infrequent visitor is simply to crate or isolate the dog well
before his or her arrival, thereby avoiding any awkwardness.
A third option, of course, might be just to make your home an
advice-free zone: just kidding, Uncle Walter!

PROBLEM #2: MY DOG BARKS

*("All day long, he just won't shut up. I'm so sick of it. I yell
at him to stop and he keeps going, and my neighbors are going
ballistic, and I just want some peace and quiet, and . . .")*

I hear your pain. Or at least I hear tell of it about ten times a
week. Dogs who bark constantly are right up there with crying babies and a leaky septic tank when it comes to making
you the most popular kid on the block. Some people can tune
it out, but I'm guessing you're not in that 0.1 percent.

Dogs bark for many reasons. They bark to alert us to danger; they bark to communicate to other dogs and animals; and
they bark, sometimes, just because they have a song in their
hearts. And howling—that even more euphonious cry—is not
limited to beagles and Nordic breeds, as some imagine. Any
breed with reasonable pipes can develop a good strong howl.

To begin with the obvious—if your dog barks out of physical distress (e.g., he needs to go outside; he *is* outside but it's
too cold; he is inside and it's too hot; he is outside and getting
rained on; he is inside and he *wants* to be outside getting
rained on) well, then simply giving him what he wants (or

relieving him of what he doesn't) is really the simplest, most effective remedy. His *are* basic animal needs, and if yours were ignored, eventually you'd be barking too.

Boredom and loneliness, too, often lead to incessant barking; if you think that's the cause, spend some quality time together (remember, it's one of the best conditions for training). Sometimes a new toy and some shared merriment will have him "purring like a kitten." Most times, however, it's not that simple. Dogs bark at squirrels, traffic, people at the door, people walking by the house. Really outrageous stuff (to you!) but in the dog's mind, vitally important. Here's how you can put a muzzle on that bark, short of actually using one.

First, stop yelling! The dog thinks you are barking, too, and are joining him in his lament. The next step is to startle your dog so that he is silent long enough to hear you when you start to use the new command "Enough!" The means needn't be elaborate—banging two pots together, clapping your hands, dropping a book, whatever he least expects. Keep in mind your dog's sensitivity level: You want him startled, not palpitating. When the dog stops barking, as if to say, "Huh?" you say, "Enough!" in a firm command voice, nothing more dramatic—he just needs to take it in. If he starts up again, startle again. Try this a few times and see what happens, but be forewarned: Champion barkers and especially dominant dogs rarely fold under this correction.

Traditionally, breaking the barker has been a long test of wills, with a huge backlash potential. If the dog knows you make the continual correction when he is merely trying to express himself, if he hears you speak to him in anger every time he opens his mouth (such as the average sleep-deprived human can rarely refrain from doing), he *may* stop the barking while you are in the room, but will more than likely resume when you aren't around. However, silencing the bark—or trying to by such means—can ruin your relationship, as he becomes conditioned to tune you out. That's why, though I'm old-fashioned at heart, I've never found anything as effective as those new high-tech bark collars now sold all over the country in pet stores and by mail order. There are different mechanisms with these: Some emit a tone, inaudible (to us) but uncomfortable to a dog's ear (the sweet sound of justice?); some spray pungent citronella up the dog's neck; some emit a mild static shock. All, however, are set off by the dog's barking. To enable you not to be totally despotic, some collars give you the option of allowing a few barks and then setting the unit to correct on the fifth or sixth bark, for example. The best feature of all, however, is that the dog does not perceive you as the agent of his correction. If you decide to travel this route of a better life through science, do consult a trainer with experience using these collars before purchasing one. He or she can advise you as to what manner of deterrent would best suit your particular dog. Many collars come with precise instructions and even a videotape, but it's always wise to customize when dealing with electronic devices.

PROBLEM #3: MY DOG DIGS
(And digs and digs and digs and digs . . .)

Next to barking, people find digging the most maddening form of excess. In the morning, you leave a landscaped, manicured backyard. In the evening, your yard looks like someone is installing a new septic field. Your dog is not only too exhausted to play but looks to be in need of yet another bath. You feel those two little veins on the side of your neck begin to bulge and wonder why you never considered sea monkeys as a better pet option.

Before we can fix this miner mania, we must ascertain *why* the dog is digging. Rule out "because he hates me" and "because I stopped giving him canned food." They might seem like reasons, but they're not. Dogs dig either because they are looking for something (searchers), trying to bury something (hoarders), or just to pass the time (bored-ers). A few even dig to escape, but unless relations with you have hit rock-bottom and his excavations are near the fence, that theory, too, is a goner.

The Searchers

The Searchers are busy creatures. Their motto is: "Leave no clump of dirt or lawn unturned." Admire their dedication, but banish the behavior. First, buy a few of the new toys such as the Buster Cube, the ball in a ball; or meld a toy with a treat—fill a Kong toy with peanut butter and a biscuit and freeze it or put a slit in a tennis ball and stick a dog cookie in it. Toys with greater challenge or reward potential may soak up his boundless energy.

When you're in a hole, stop digging, or so the saying goes. So, second, consider how you have previously responded when your dog has tried to burrow his way to China. You probably filled the hole back up with the same dirt. Very thoughtful: ready for him to have another go at it. Maybe, no, PROBABLY, you have gone out on occasion and given the dog a good what for. What did that accomplish? Well, your dog is probably careful not to dig in front of you. Was that ever the problem? Nothing gained if he resumes the excavation as soon as your tires hit the pavement.

As with barking, the most effective correction for a compulsive undesirable behavior is not a scolding or a tugging. You'd be scolding and tugging him every waking minute, and he would take a dim view of it—and you. Better if the correction doesn't seem to come from you at all, but rather from "above" (cue *The Twilight Zone* theme here)! Actually, in this case the correction will come from below. Instead of filling the holes with dirt, pick up whatever poop is in your yard and fill the hole with that! Cover with an inch or so of topsoil and then just wait for your dog to dig. Dogs HATE having poop on their paws, so this is a great deterrent. You'll probably have to do this in a few different locations until he concludes that poop is lurking under every blade of grass in your yard. Now, this tactic assumes he is digging normal dog-sized holes. If he seems to be planning an Olympic-sized pool, you will definitely not have enough poop to fill the hole, even if you take up a collection from the neighbors. Would you really want to live near a manure pile anyway? A final word on the scatological approach: If your dog has the misfortune of suffering from coprophagy (better known as a taste for eating poop), do NOT try the poop deterrent, as the hole would be seen as a sort of covered-dish buffet—let's just not go there. . . .

For such dogs, and for dogs with owners not prepared to shovel feces for a good cause, one can substitute really cheap thin-skinned balloons. You blow them up as big as they can be without popping, and put them in the hole, covering them with a bit of dirt. Stand back and watch the fireworks. Once the dirt starts blowing up in his face, your dog will think better of digging. You may have to plant a few mines to make the dog believe there's no safe place to dig in your yard, but eventually he will. **CAUTION:** Be extremely careful your dog does not eat the balloons once they're popped! Latex is *not* on his diet and could be extremely harmful to him.

Chicken Out

If you happen to have a dog who doesn't mind poop on his paws or exploding balloons (or, heaven forbid, LIKES one or both of those options), you are then left with the chicken-wire solution. Yes, chicken wire. The sensation a dog gets when he digs into wire is one that, forgive me, he won't dig. So he won't. Dig. Anyway, if you find yourself without chickens and a henhouse, please proceed directly to your nearest Home-Do-It-Yourself-with-Lots-of-Help-and-then-Hire-a-Contractor-to-Fix-It-Anyway store. Buy a good-sized roll of chicken wire, based on the size of your dog's holes. There's no scientific measurement for this, so overbuy and maybe you can get some chickens if there's enough left over. Next, put your dog in the house (so that he can't see what you're doing), and place a ball of chicken wire in each hole. Cover the hole with dirt and let your dog back into the yard as you go inside to watch the festivities.

The Hoarders

If at any point in your life as a dog owner you've lost something inside the house only to find it somewhere in the backyard, you most likely have been the victim of "the hoarder." If you are lucky, your hoarder "buries" his trophies *indoors.* This improves the chances of seeing your belongings again, and is to be preferred (except for when your mother-in-law starts rearranging the couch cushion and discovers a pair of your thong underwear). The less lucky will be digging outside for their socks. I've broken the hoarders into a few subgroups:

Hoarders who love the drama: If you routinely race after your dog when you see him take off with your stuff, and, being late for some engagement yet missing a critical wardrobe element (such as the aforementioned thong), you rush out into the yard screaming, "Okay, dog-boy, where is it?" you could very well be playing into his idea of a good time. Maybe he has been seeing less of you lately—maybe he has never seen enough. Either way, he has found a foolproof way of commanding your undivided attention. So what to do? First, you need to keep your stuff put away, which sounds deceptively simple, I know. The dog should also be supervised constantly, which means that if you are unable to be in the same room with him, he should be crated or confined to a small area. Think about using your laundry room, the kitchen, anywhere his kleptomaniacal tendencies cannot be readily indulged. *Then* you need to give the dog some added attention and maybe even a new toy or two. During this training period, I would allow the dog outside only when I could be outside with him. That way, if he starts looking for a spot to dig, you can take preemptive action. In this case, a correction could be anything from a verbal "ah-ah" to throwing a soda-can bomb (that's a soda can that contains only a few pennies and has been taped shut. See "Plan B" on page 203 for a full explanation on the creation and proper use of a startler) *not* at the dog, but in his general direction. (Most disarming! Just keep it concealed and silent until you hurl it—you don't want to be ID'd as the agent of the correction here.) Or you could just watch with rapt attention as she discovers one of the booby-traps previously described (heh, heh, heh).

The dog who really covets a possession: I have one of these.

When I give my Border collie Trigger a bone, she paces for fifteen to twenty minutes, trying out various hiding places for it. She goes behind the couch, behind the chair, under the cushions, in a corner. Eventually the urge to splurge overtakes her, and she just starts chewing it. Perhaps if this behavior had been limited to *her* toys I wouldn't have needed to change it, but she would do likewise with laundry and the kids' toys, so it had to be stopped. If this is your situation, control the environment! I would never give Triggs a bone outside because I know she would bury it in a heartbeat. She can have it only when she's in the TV room and only when I am with her. That way, I can nip any truly potentially destructive behavior in the bud. If the bone made her lose all sense, then I would either give it to her only in her crate or take it out of her life completely. That actually sounds more Draconian than it is: She would forget all about it in a day or so, provided it was really OUT of her life and not simply on top of the refrigerator! Come on, that's the first place anyone would look, and besides, she can see it! I have a student with five Parson Russell terriers who are so crazy about tennis balls that she has to keep them in a secure location to preserve her sanity. If she put the balls anywhere that the dogs could see or smell them, they would bark and leap in the air until she gave them up. One day she hit upon the inspired idea of hiding them in the refrigerator. Her dogs can't see OR smell them, and as long as she hides them when the dogs are in the other room she is home free. Her friends and family are so used to this that they now think nothing of rolling the tennis balls aside to get to the orange juice!

Dogs Who Are Bored and the Landscapers Who Love Them

Now here's an important caveat: If you suspect your dog feels neglected and digging is his way of letting you know that, then you'd be well advised to spend more time with him in addition to implementing the previous suggestions. You took him from the company of his own kind, so you've got to take up the emotional slack. In Florida I had a student with a beautiful German shepherd. His biggest problem was that the dog dug holes in the yard. I interrogated him at length about his schedule and face time with the dog, and though he admitted to being a busy guy, the dog, he insisted, was well loved and had the lion's share of his attention. Seeing as neglect was not an issue, I suggested he try the balloon-in-the-hole trick. When I arrived at his house five days later, there was a large landscaping truck parked in front of his house loaded with sod, and I briefly wondered which of his neighbors, all with lovely lawns like his, could be having their yard done. When I walked into the backyard, I had my answer: *His* yard was being resodded. All of it. It was a somber tale. The owner had been invited to go to Key West for the weekend. The neighbor's boy was going to come over twice a day to feed the dog, who was being confined to the house and backyard. Before leaving, and without the dog's having seen him, the man took the measure of planting about ten balloons. Apparently the neighbor's boy never ventured into the backyard when he came over to the owner's house. If he had, he would have noticed that the dog was systematically tearing out every blade of grass in an attempt to find more "balloon friends." The strategy had backfired. The dog, naturally game and starved for some form of interaction, had found a reward in the loud pop of the bursting balloon. One man's meat is another man's poison. But to this German shepherd, that was entertainment! His owner was not so entertained, however, and agreed, after settling the landscaper's fee, to make some major improvements in the amount and quality of interaction with his dog. Now he routinely takes the dog running with him and to a nearby field for a rigorous game of fetch. And if he can't give the dog such quality time on a given day, he hires the neighborhood kids to come over for a good old-fashioned canine triathlon around the yard. The owner happily reports that his pricey lawn has never since gone to seed!

PROBLEM #4: MY DOG CHEWS THINGS HE SHOULDN'T

(Or, Learning the hard way why half a pair of shoes is not better than none!)

For the most part, chewing is normal. I know reading this makes you want to run naked right out into the streets and scream, but it's true. And, as you probably know, dogs chew whatever they can get their teeth into. It's in their contract.

You have oral fixations of your own, I'm sure. But when people have the urge to chew, they don't grab someone's shoe and start gnawing on it. Usually, they settle for a piece of gum, a toothpick, a pencil, or perhaps a cigar. All deplorable habits in my book, but still acceptable by human standards. So, we have two issues here with the dogs—the urge to chew (which is not limited to their species) and a lack of judgment as to what is acceptable to chew on. When (not if) you have ever caught your dog chewing on something precious to you, you've come to know the five stages of grief: *denial*—"That *can't* be my new Kate Spade handbag!"; *sadness*—"Oh, my God, he even chewed off the label"; *anger*—"I am going to kill this dog, my husband who made us buy it, the breeder who sold it, and everyone in the breeder's extended family"; *acceptance*—"Well, my birthday *is* coming up and this *is* my husband's dog and *he is* the one who forgot to put Jaws in the crate"; *commitment to training the dog*—"I'm going right out to buy a copy of *Kathy Santo's Dog Sense!*" (You go, girl!)

All right, let's get to work, starting with: *Why* do dogs chew? Lots of reasons—boredom, teething, excess energy, even—and often—stress. What stress could a dog have, you ask? Familial discord, moving, kids gone to college (yours, not his), a new puppy or baby in the family—these are just a few possible sources of anxiety for him. What are *not* reasons for chewing? Spite for your being out late last night; to punish you for forgetting his good-night dog cookie; and, least of all, to make all of your new underwear look like it got caught in the weed eater. This isn't personal, and dogs who chew are not *trying* to send you a message!

That's Entertainment

The first thing to do is to assemble a good variety of chew toys and rotate them every week or two. Toys should be geared toward the intensity of the chewer, so don't pick a plush toy for a T. rex unless you want it to be turned to lint overnight. (My husband has suggested it would be more efficient and cheaper just to give our most chewy dog wads of ten-dollar bills.) Serious chewers require heavy-duty toys—Nylabones, Nylabone Galileo bones, *sterilized* real bones (from pet suppliers only. Homemade bones can potentially splinter and be harmful to dogs!), plastic Tuffy Balls, Kong toys, etc. Kongs and real bones can be stuffed with things like peanut butter or dog cookies, providing extra motivation to chew on the toy and not, say, a Gucci loafer. I use peanut butter and then put the chew treat in the freezer, making a sort of peanut pop— irresistible! As do jumpers, chewers need some toys that come out only when you have guests. These toys are superspecial, such as a Kong full of something he would deem gourmet stuffing: It keeps the nervous energy typical of chewers focused on something other than the guests, although even a dog who's part piranha will very rarely start gnawing spontaneously on a visitor's leg. Those of you with dogs who chew with their right pinkie extended, so to speak, can gloat as you buy little Steiff toys and all those adorable colored bones for your genteel chewers while the rest of us consider salvaged auto parts. Just remember that however meek or mighty your dog's chops may be, the problem is the same: Boredom and stress are usually at the root of compulsive chewing, so, in the long run, exercise and training will go a long way toward eliminating the problem at its source. But meanwhile . . .

Collect

Now that your dog has appropriate chew toys, your next job is to put any inappropriate ones out of reach. All of you with children, just stop laughing now! I know you can't remember what color carpet you have for all the the layers of toys strewn across the floor, but if you want to fight this battle, you'll have to rally the troops and institute martial law. If your kids can't be enlisted to help save your shoes, perhaps you should inform them that their cooperation could help save your dog. One of my students had a Parson Russell terrier who would try to eat anything that hit the floor. Her alimentary credits included a pair of socks and a twenty-dollar bill. One day, during one of my private lessons with the owner and the dog, she started acting strange and finally threw up one of his daughter's hair bands. The family had seen the dog scarf it the night before and, having grown accustomed to a dog that would probably eat fire given the chance, they assumed the hair accessory would pass right through her in a day or so. In fact, had it begun traveling through her intestines, surgery would certainly have been needed to remove it. The whole family got the message and immediately changed priorities. They initiated a policy of zero tolerance for dropping or leaving things on the floor. With stepped-up training and dutifully rotated designated chew toys, eventually the potentially lethal behavior was broken. Don't wait for your dog to cough up a Honda before you decide there is more at stake here than your wardrobe.

Confinement

Confinement was recommended for the Hoarder (see "The Hoarders" in the Problem #3 section, page 195), and, being one of most versatile of behavioral remedies, it may help you tame the chew hound, too. If you can't supervise your chewer, keep him crated or in some small area, with nothing but his own toys to chew on.

So while you adjust his training regimen, your preemptive-action mantra should be: Entertain, collect, and confine. Entertain, collect, and confine.

"But what should I do if I actually *catch* him in the act of stealing something?" I'm glad you asked. First, give the dog a verbal "ah-ah," which should at the very least make him turn around to look at you. Do not yell, and especially do not yell,

"NO!" Expressions of anger promote fear, which effectively prevents the dog from taking instruction. Like a superpop on the leash, an angry response to incorrect behavior does more to disorient than to instruct. In fact, chronic verbal abuse can lead to a variety of fear-based behaviors far more bothersome than chewing. These include submissive urination, panicked biting, and running away. If you have made any progress in training, angry yelling is the most efficient way to kiss it good-bye. Since most people don't know how to say no without heat, as their kids will attest, I recommend "ah-ah," an unusual sound your dog knows to be just for him and one difficult to pronounce with true heat.

Okay, back to the scene of the crime. You've just caught the dog in the act and said "ah-ah," causing him to stop and look at you. Now what are you gonna do? Approach the dog calmly and take the object, say, your daughter's numbered, signed, and retired Beanie Baby, from his mouth and—here's the crucial part—replace it with something he *should* be chewing. Then you can praise him for chewing the right thing (rather than berate him for chewing the wrong one). Got the picture? But, you ask, "What would any training be without distractions?" My, you have come far! Therefore, go now and place that same Beanie Baby before him and see what he does. Yes, take it out of the protective cube: no guts, no glory. If your dog is one of the few who can't even look at the Beanie Baby now because of the aforementioned "ah-ah" followed by the redirection to the other toy, go out tonight and buy a lottery ticket based on his birthday-date digits—you are one lucky training team! Most dogs will go right for that Beanie Baby yet again. So why go through the drill? Because that's training. As with your dog's learning desirable behaviors, his unlearning the undesirable ones requires your patience and gradual escalation of deterrence until you find the minimum effective force. You can always step it up and continue teaching, but once you've overdone it (as with screaming, "NO!") the learning has ceased. And he may be scarred for life. If you've never heard of psychiatrists for canines, I can assure you that they aren't hurting for business, and they don't take insurance. Stick with the program, and you'll save money in the long run. Go ahead and try the "ah-ah," plus toy redirection, one more time to be sure that that method won't work. If it does, count your blessings and proceed to the Problem #5 section. If it doesn't, implement Plan B.

Plan B

So your dog won't take a hint. Time to use your superior intellect once again. (You've always got that to fall back on!) Like immoderate digging, incessant chewing can be addressed with the scare tactic. Today's arts-and-crafts project is a dog trainer's version of the stun grenade, but really we're only trying to startle your pet. Something as innocuous as a balled-up pair of socks will do the trick for a sound- or emotionally sensitive dog (unless they are his ultimate chew fetish). For others, a small beanbag or ring of keys does the trick. If your dauntless dog requires the Humvee of projectile startling, try the pennies in the soda can with the spout taped shut. He won't know what hit him, but remember, WE DO NOT AIM TO HIT. Whatever the projectile (and once again the choice is guided by an ever-growing understanding of your dog's personality), it must land in his vicinity, not on any part of his body. Now be honest with yourself: If you're a total spaz and couldn't hit the side of a doghouse, don't take chances. Let someone with an arm do the pitching. But if you're a competent hurler . . .

Place the Beanie Baby on open ground and camouflage yourself behind the couch or a door—remain out of sight but within observation range. Wait until the dog picks up or starts to paw the Beanie Baby and immediately launch projectile. While he's still startled, rush in like the cavalry and save the day: "Pookiebear, what happened to you?" (Here, a little whiny talk increases the anxiety level of the event and makes the impression more memorable.) If he could talk, Pookiebear would be saying, "Man, that noise almost scared the poop out of me. I was standing here, minding my own business, about to chew this thing, when BAM!" The key here is the anonymous correction. Pookiebear mustn't think, "What, are you crazy, throwing those keys at me? I'm calling Animal Protection!" He must never know you're behind his distress. It was not a correction in that sense, but a random, senseless act. If you repeat the startle, after the second or third time, he'll see that the event is not so random but the result of picking up that infernal Beanie Baby, which doesn't seem worth such upset. When he catches on to this fact, change the location and change the bait. With most dogs, it shouldn't take more than two or three tries at the appropriate correction level to get them to expect an explosion whenever they reach for the wrong toy and kick the chaw habit.

But suppose you haven't hit that level yet. If your startle doesn't startle—or worse, it becomes an object of play in itself—escalate to a louder correction. Can of pennies not doing it? How about slamming a pair of pot lids? One student had to drop a metal folding chair to persuade his dog not to chew the molding off the walls. (You think you have problems?) The dubious achievement award, however, goes to the family fed up with their toy poodle's taste for antique Persian rugs. For Frenchie, key chains and cans full of coins were like music to chew by, so was virtually every other cacophony until the family resorted to a boat horn. Unfortunately by the time they discovered this effective correction, a family heirloom had been reduced to a colorful dish towel. (There can be a price to pay for escalating correction intensity too slowly, but it's preferable to going too fast, at least from the training perspective.) The only living casualty of this tactic was the owner's visiting mother-in-law, who had not been informed aforehand of the intended strike. By her own account to the EMTs, she'd just been sitting there minding her own business when . . . Oh well, you can't think of everything.

PROBLEM #5: MY DOG DOESN'T LISTEN TO ME
(Lost in translation)

Before you make this serious charge, try two things. First, have your dog's hearing checked. If that's fine, try saying something he can understand. I'm not cracking wise. Owners who lodge the my-dog-doesn't-listen complaint have typically taken very few pains to teach the dog comprehensible commands. A dog can understand only the handful of words you have taught him, and that's a well-trained dog. Everything else you say is pure gibberish, unless you show him what you mean.

Any idiot can try to train a dog without attempting communication. There are those familiar types who yell "SIT" at the dog, who may or may not be motivated to understand what the owner wanted. When the dog doesn't sit, the "trainer" gives him a good jerk on the chain. If there is still no sit, the command becomes progressively louder until the dog either sits (quite by chance) or bites the guy (which would not be unwarranted). After a few attempts like this, the dog may actually start responding to the command, but is this training? Not really. You may believe you have programmed a few commands, but how will you test them if fear is the sole basis for his obedience? Fear can condition you not to do some things, but it's a terribly inefficient way to learn. A well-trained dog is more than a collection of severe corrections and attendant neuroses. A well-trained dog has learned to understand.

A little empathy across the species divide will serve you well. Imagine yourself in a foreign country, asking for directions and not being understood at all. Now imagine that the foreign friend you were meant to visit doesn't even try to help you understand what he is saying but rather repeats the same instructions in his own tongue with rising impatience and even aggression. Now imagine that your friend slaps a collar and leash on you and starts jerking you around. Next time, you're going to Disneyland. It is perfectly possible to communicate with your dog, but to do so requires that you patiently teach him a few words in your language and apply yourself to learning a few expressions in his. Only then can you distinguish between a dog who doesn't know what you want and a dog who knows very well but is distracted or, to borrow a phrase, doesn't listen. The former needs to be retrained with positive motivation; the latter needs the benefit of measured correction.

A Failure to Communicate

Do you blather? Perhaps you are very eloquent at making your desires known to your fellow humans, but how are you at speaking to your dog? Some diagnostics:

Do your commands typically contain at least ten words? ("Sit! Come on, you know how to sit! Hold still, I need to put your leash on. When I say 'sit,' I mean 'sit!' ")

Do you solicit your dog's opinion? ("How's that new food, Old Yeller? Yucky, huh? Yeah, I didn't think Mommie's little boy would like that, no, I didn't. Maybe I could put a little macaroni and cheese on it to make it all better, huh? Whaddya say?")

Who could listen to that all day? Certainly not a dog. People who engage in blather often form the false impression that the dog understands and is therefore "listening" sometimes and choosing not to listen at others. Typically such people have been deceived by the power of tone to influence a dog's behavior. For example:

"It's okay, Fang. Daddy knows you didn't mean to rip out all the flowers. You were just looking for your Nylabone, I didn't mean to yell at you and hurt your feelings. You're a good boy. You won't do that again, right? Right? Yes, that's a good boy."

Moments earlier, Daddy was bawling Fang out for making mulch of the prizewinning roses. That damage is done, both the horticultural and the psychological. Fang doesn't know what he did wrong, but the sting of the tirade remains (minimal learning; maximum anxiety). Now, to make matters worse, Daddy is making it up to Fang for having bawled him out just moments earlier. Fang, because he hears such a reassuring tone, naturally responds warmly and affirmatively, giving Daddy to believe that the lesson has been accepted. Who's got the IQ deficit here? To find out, wait and see what Daddy does when Fang does his thing in the garden next time.

Or consider an example of good programming totally mucked up by carelessness. You have taken almost two weeks to teach Upton that "down" means "down." Whenever, wherever. In a plane, on a train—you remember the drill. Anyway, you're meticulous about practicing and correcting him in training, to the point that he knows what "down" really means. Then the day after they've delivered your new leather couch you enter a state of near hysteria when you see Upton trying it out for comfort. You scream, "Down!" and he plops himself down on Auntie Fi who's sitting on the end watching *Jeopardy!* ("What is *Kathy Santo's Dog Sense?*"). Auntie Fi may not have gotten that one right, but Upton did. As you pull him off the couch, yelling, "When I say 'DOWN,' I mean 'DOWN!' " all he can think is, "Has she finally lost it? I did 'down.' But you can bet I won't be making that mistake again." Old habits die hard, but hard-won training can fade in an instant. No matter the circumstances, be careful of what you ask for, especially in the early days of training before your dog gets used to reading your mind.

It's a proven fact that the more unresponsive the dog, the more verbose a blatherer becomes; the more unresponsive the dog, on and on in a vicious cycle. That said, one must acknowledge that dogs are actually great listeners, if you speak consistently and concisely. A command is a word or two. It is preceded by the dog's name. If he understands it, you are communicating; if he does not, you are taking shots in the dark, with correspondingly spotty results. I don't make combinations of contradictory words. For instance, you teach a dog "sit" and "down." What do you expect when you command him to "sit down"? Or as we say up here in the Northeast, "siddown." This is not to say relations must be so curt. When I am hanging out with my dog Trigger, I'll say things like "Hey, Triggs, how ya doin'? Where's your ball? Go find it." And Trigger, appreciating my pleasant tone, will wag her tail, give me a million kisses, and perhaps even go find her ball. Is she "listening"? No, but we're just hanging out, so who cares? If, however, we were outside and I observed her stalking a squirrel, the conversation would be "TRIGGS, HERE!" There would be no room for doubt in her (TRIGGS's) mind that I wanted her to come to me ("HERE"). Since I have taught the "here" command with a multitude of variables, no matter what else is going on around us, Triggs knows that those words oblige her to wheel around and come to me. If she doesn't, she can expect to be corrected. That's the deal, and that deal, which also includes love, care, and trust, is the cornerstone of a good training relationship. Is she listening? Let's just say we have an understanding.

PROBLEM #6: MY DOG CHARGES THROUGH DOORS
("Comin' throooough")

Unless your dog works for the ATF, the DEA, or the FBI, charging through doors is a problem and should be fixed. Dogs who bust past and into people to get through the door ahead of them have leadership issues. Perhaps you have ceded management authority to your dog in the past, but take this little quiz to determine who is the real alpha dog in your household.

1. Which of you pays the rent or mortgage?
2. Who pays the water bill?
3. Who buys the dog food?

If you did not answer "the dog" in at least one case, you are probably the alpha dog with all the perks and privileges of the position, including the largely ceremonial though still much appreciated right to be first going through the door.

Dogs who rush the door are a danger not only to the people they may tackle along the way, but also to themselves. I think not only of the haunted-house scenario in which a ghoul might be lurking behind the most innocuous-looking door (the celebrated cartoon hound Scooby Doo was known not only for his capacity to mumble a fair amount of English, but also for having the cunning never to be first across the threshold). More practically, there are the countless cases of dogs who, seeing the door left ajar, have taken it as an invitation to bound into the street and into traffic. The solution here is not better animation, but a two-step correction: first, we want to deprogram the "door opens–dog bolts" reflex; second, we want to teach a "door opens–dog sits and waits" response. You have presumably already taught your dog the "sit-wait" command. So what you need to do for the second step is to introduce the open door as a distraction. Give him the "sit-wait" command as you practice opening the door. Eventually you can eliminate the verbal command (as you did when moving to the pure hand signal for the down) so that the opening of the door will in effect become a command to sit.

But first things first. How do we extinguish the urge to rush the door?

Unknowingly, most owners have taught their dogs to go through doors ahead of them. In fact, a dog's first experiences with humans' portals is typically of being hurried through one on the way to the nearest patch of grass where he can take care of business. Once that pattern is established, the dog continues to conform, making for the door as soon as the leash appears. The owner can barely stretch an arm ahead of the determined canine, and has scarcely turned the knob before the dog bolts. As with any undesirable behavior, tolerating it is virtually as good as training your dog to do it, each uncorrected instance only confirming his sense that he's acting properly. Here's how we put the brakes on. Start with the dog on leash and tell him it's "time to go outside" or whatever you normally say. Keep the slack on the leash short (one to two feet) and approach the door. SLOWLY begin to open it, but no more than an inch. When your dog starts to exhibit the frantic behavior (pawing the door frame for a wider passage, shoving his nose in the crack), IMMEDIATELY slam the door shut and say nothing. Your dog may become even more excited, or, more likely, he'll be stunned by the odd turn of events. Now, repeat the same drill—slowly opening the door just an inch, slamming it at the first sign of frenzy. Perverse though this may seem (to him), the point is simply to startle him into an aware-ness that doors can bite. If his nose gets caught in a pinch as he tries to barrel through, that's okay. A bump on the nose hurts less than being hit by a car after bounding unobstructed through the door. Still, the force of the slam must be gauged according to three factors: first, his size (toy dogs obviously require a lighter touch than large breeds); second, his physical sensitivity; and third, the dog's perception of your action. If your Labrador decides it's fun to dodge the zany slamming door, perhaps next time a bit more force (and a wee nip at his nose or paw or whatever part he tries to intrude first) is called for to show him that this isn't a game. After a few rounds of this, your dog should show some signs of wariness about the formerly innocuous door. Once the mania gives way to more composed circumspection at the sight of the one-inch opening, add another inch. Then another. Soon the door will be wide open, whereupon, if he has kept his cool, tell him, "Okay, let's go," and allow him through. The key: YOU tell him when it's right to proceed. If you have already taught the "sit-wait," it should now even be possible, using that command, for you to precede your dog through the door. Just remember that any regression to threshold frenzy will be your prompt to resume slamming. But don't pare back by inches: You have to go back to a closed door and start all over—sorry! I imagine you are saying, "Hmm, this could take some time." It could, and for that reason, do not try to teach this modification before an actual scheduled outing, when your dog's bladder is full. This is only a drill, but an important refinement in the training regimen.

PROBLEM #7: MY DOG BEGS AT THE TABLE

("More, please?")

Oliver Twist has nothing on some of the serious canine mooches I have known. Sad eyes, cocked heads, sighs, moans, the "drool me a river" jowls—and those are the subtle ones.

The truly over-the-top food beggars often appear to have had more Method acting than basic training, pawing your legs, barking angstfully, and feigning starvation. Whatever the individual style, however, the behavior is universally irritating. To fix it, though, first consider how it started.

Ninety percent of serious begging disorders are made, not born. At some time, after smelling something interesting and seeing you sit down at the table (as you are wont to do), your dog has come over and sat beside the table. On this occasion, someone gave the dog some food, and overnight, a star is born. The (human) misdeed is done with varying degrees of culpability. Sometimes the erring party is a kid who doesn't know better. Sometimes it's a pathetic adult trying to curry favor with the dog. (Houseguests are common perpetrators of this variety, but I have yet to meet one who would own up to it.)

Very often it's the innocent who are guilty. A dog can develop an unfortunate taste for people food just by spending a few hours with a toddler. When toddlers toddle around the house, they often carry food on their hands or clothes. (The resulting dog behavior is often mistaken for affection.) The high-chair area is ground zero for the development of severe begging disorders. The dog becomes the child's best friend as soon as the little tyke starts pitching food, which not only sends the dog into a frenzy of dancing and licking the floor, but also elicits from the no-less-frenzied parent the desperate cry of "Nooooooo!" (only slightly more effective in controlling misbehavior of toddlers than it is with dogs).

If you have a small child, the first step toward taking back dinnertime is to remove the dog when you are feeding the child. Confine him to another room, crate him—whatever is necessary to put him out of range of tasty projectiles.

If you don't have a child, make sure the dog is out of sight any time you are doing some particular kinetic cooking— flipping pancakes, stir-frying, what have you. Only then can you initiate remedial training.

The next thing you have to do is go to the "Teaching 'Down' " section of the book (page 102) and train your dog to do a down-wait. As with dogs who rush at doors, dogs who beg are responding to a deeply ingrained motivation. The habit is therefore similarly time-consuming to break. Maybe more so: For many dogs, food is the mother of all motivators, and therefore a heck of a distraction. So be patient when you teach your dog what is, in effect, a down-wait with food as the distraction factor.

Do start his training under sane circumstances, not just hours before serving holiday dinner for twelve. The first test involves only him doing a down-wait as you sit at the table having a cup of tea and dry toast. Build up to more people and better food, following the basic distraction rules for a "down-wait" as you would with any other command. Eventually your dog should be able to bear watching you eat. But remember, the dog who calmly stays near the dinner table doesn't want the food any less; he is simply overcoming his undesirable impulses, thanks to training. So stock up on the "Quicker Picker-Upper" all the same—the begging may stop but not the drooling.

PROBLEM #8: MY DOG STEALS THINGS

(From countertops, tabletops, laptops . . . a thief in the night, day, and afternoon)

Now you see it, now you don't. Whether your dog is stealing papers from your desk, dish towels, or marinated flank steaks on their way to the grill, a thief is a thief. Stealing is a form of compulsive behavior, like the proverbial digging to China. And even if the stolen item is food, the misdeed may have as much to do with the pleasure of taking it as the thrill of consuming it.

Go back to "Problem #4: My Dog Chews Things He Shouldn't" (page 199) for some basic strategies. Consider whether the dog isn't acting up out of boredom in an attempt to get you to play the universally popular Chase the Dog to Get Back Your Stuff game. Fortunately, you already know what to do about that. Then implement basic preventive measures, such as collecting (things) and confining (the dog). The Plan B solution (see page 203) of startling the chronic chew hound can also be applied to the kleptomaniac. It's the strategy of making the misbehavior unpleasant rather than teaching an alternative behavior as we did with Problem #7.

The approach with a stealer involves a sting operation wherein the dog is lured into making a mistake precisely so that we can implement the correction. Since this method is all bite and no reward, the key is to dissociate yourself from the correction. For instance, try leaving a bologna sandwich on the countertop and then disappear while remaining within observation range. Let your dog go in to investigate. As with any stakeout, patience is key: You must nail him in the act, not merely at the scene of the crime. Wait until he actually makes for the sandwich before launching the startler. Be aware that you'll need to experiment with the startler's intensity. What may deter him from stealing your cable bill may not work with the bologna sandwich. Some dogs, especially the more dominant ones, will tough out a thunderclap if the booty is choice enough.

Booby-trapping the object of theft is also effective. If the dish towel is his quarry, wrapping your keys in same may be just the unwelcome surprise to scare him straight. If he is a food thief, my favorite move is the "Tabasco, or Grannick's Bitter Apple, or volcano salsa" sandwich placed at the edge of a counter, which a student recently served with great success to her standard poodle. Booby traps are especially helpful in establishing plausible deniability. The dog never suspects it's you, and so your relationship is untarnished, even benefiting from your big entrance as white knight at the moment of his distress. ("Does Fifi need something to wash that down with?")

For dogs who resist the most startling of startlers, electronic devices are, once again, the final frontier. These range from the collars we have discussed to wired mats for countertops. Again, they are perfectly safe and effective, but should be used only after all alternatives have been attempted and under the guidance of an experienced professional.

PROBLEM #9: MY DOG ACTS LIKE A MANIAC WHEN GREETING ME, MY FAMILY, AND ANYONE WHO COMES THROUGH THE DOOR
(How to lose kin and influence people)

This problem is such a headache, I bundled it together with Problem #1. See page 185 for solutions, unless you prefer living alone.

PROBLEM #10: MY DOG CHEWS HIS LEASH WHILE IT'S ATTACHED TO HIS COLLAR
(And it's a leather leash from Coach)

This leash-chewing syndrome is common among dogs belonging to people who start stories by moaning, "So I bought a two-hundred-dollar white T-shirt for my toddler to wear to a barbecue. . . ." The toddler, having no idea where his mouth really is, immediately turns the white T-shirt into a piece of wearable art. The dog, who chews everything that doesn't chew him first, is outfitted with a beautiful, expensive Coach leather leash. You know what happens next. You know because you have both pieces of the leash to prove it.

Many dogs chew their leashes, but your dog's particular reason depends on who he is. If he's the dominant type, the chewing and tugging are likely a means of controlling the walk. And you. If he is particularly timid (less common among chewers) it may be a displacement of nervous energy produced by being out and about. (Reassurance should help here.) If your dog is simply full of beans, however, the chewing may be a form of play behavior. Attempts to correct this in the past may have been misinterpreted or, the correction being unenforced ('fess up!), may have simply been ignored. Then there are those dogs who chew everything all the time, as we have dealt with in the discussion of Problem #4 (see page 199).

Happily, leash chewing is a behavior that can be fixed

regardless of personality type and motivation. Ultimately, the correction will depend on training an alternative (less destructive) behavior, so that a "sit" command, for instance, may be given every time he attempts to chew the leash. In the interim, however, an ounce of deterrence is worth a pound of cure. Coming to the rescue here is our old friend Grannick's Bitter Apple, applied to the leash when he isn't looking (as with all unpleasant surprises) just before your walk. Most will grab the leash and, tasting the bitterness, simply let go. Some will foam at the mouth and shake their heads, doing a fair impression of the rabid dog in *Old Yeller*. That's fine. Just feign the old "What happened to Sweetums?" and continue the walk. You may need to reapply the Bitter Apple, so have the bottle with you. Dogs learn most quickly when they make their own discovery, and one mouthful of foulness may be worth months of corrective tugs. If perchance Bitter Apple is entirely to your dog's taste, peppermint or hot cinnamon Binaca and Tabasco sauce is ever ready. You're bound to hit one he can't stand. Just remember to apply the substance of choice on the leash every time you walk him for the next couple of weeks. The bitter pill won't work if the leash doesn't taste consistently bad.

Dogs whose chewing is based on an oral fixation can be offered a toy or stick or ball after the leash chewing has been stopped. I owned a golden retriever whose life depended on carrying something in her mouth, or so she thought. So before we began our daily walk, I would give her a stuffed dog toy, and she would happily carry it for the entire duration of the walk. Leash chewing averted—oral fixation satisfied.

I can hear you asking, "What about chain leashes?", and yes, they work to deter the dog's chewing fixation, but they're uncomfortable to hold. Besides, we want to treat the problem, not mask the symptoms. Today it's your Coach leash; tomorrow, your Coach belt. (See, I do understand.)

CHAPTER 8

Final Words

Thoughts from the Other End of the Leash

So you've arrived at the end of the book. Unless you're one of those "read the last page first" kind of people, you now know what it takes to train YOUR dog. Not a phantom "Joe Every Dog," but your dog—the one who hates food, loves a squeaky toy named Sherman, and has the energy level of a bar of soap! And guess what. You can train him just as well as someone who has a food-driven high–energy level dog! Your training will be different, but it will suit your dog to a "T."

Also, please know that you will make mistakes in your training—it's part of YOUR learning process. Dogs retain easily and are very forgiving of your honest, well-intentioned errors.

Congratulations on making the effort to improve your relationship with your dog. That's the ultimate reward of training you've done together—the lifelong bond shared by two living beings who, hopefully by now, have a much greater understanding and respect for each other.

Happy training!

ACKNOWLEDGMENTS

In every book acknowledgment that I've ever read, the author mentions that "there are so many people I have to thank, but I can't thank them all," and yet, the writer attempts to do just that. Forgive me, but I'm about to embark on the same quest.

To my husband, Eric, who put up with my running page after page after page to him for months on end. And he still stayed married to me.

To Ryan and Elisa, my lovely, well-trained children who left me alone *and* read over my shoulder *and* created enough chaos during my "writing time" to remind me of what was really important—them!!

Heidi Osborne—training assistant, right arm, best friend, and confidante—I love you! Isn't this so much fun? Thanks for everything, including agreeing to be in all the pictures. You can change now.

Jim Osborne—where to start thanking *you*? For downloading my edits, uploading my edits, taking the pictures, downloading the pictures, retaking the pictures, re-downloading the pictures—all without a complaint. You're the best!

To Mom and Dad—without my dog Teddi, where would

the pattern of loving dogs have started? From those days came this girl! I love you both.

To Gram Russo—thanks for always letting me pet every dog we saw on our walks at the shore, even though it turned a twenty-minute walk into a two-hour one.

Arline Hall—the best proofreader and cheerleader anyone could ever ask for. You remember the "before"? The "after" is because of you, too. I love you!

Dr. Wayne Diamond, Animal Care Extraordinaire in Stuart, Florida, for reading the manuscript with a "vet's eye."

Bryna Potsdam—my heartfelt thanks for all your love and support *and* for introducing me to the wonderful people at the Treasure Coast Humane Society. They are the ones who generously allowed me to teach at their facility in Florida so that my training method could be available to everyone who adopted a shelter dog.

To Shirley and Jane Wurz—training the Sheltie kids was so much fun! The best of times, right? Thank you both for inviting me to the Humane Society's first Chocolate Festival fund-raiser. From there, the rest is history.

Harold Dow—without you (and Apollo!) there would have been none of this. Thank you! Thank you!

To everyone at Robe Imbriano's Crystal Stair TV—you all gave me the idea that my teaching method was bigger than my backyard. Robe, you believed in me and put me "out there" with some wonderful contacts. I'll never be able to thank you enough. In all that I do, I hope I'm making you proud of me!

Hugs and kisses to Carla Denaly, who loved this manuscript enough to bring it to her friend at a publishing house. You're the best.

Daryl Pendana—someone who's too cool to even *be* my friend. At this moment, I can't think of enough original words to say thank you, you know? Next time.

Rich Medina—thanks to you and the team over at Pryor Cashman—Bob Stein and Steve Huff—who made me turn in my rose-colored glasses for a pair for *reading*!!

Alvin Goldstein and Ira Altcheck—from your least knowledgeable client—thank you for always being so patient with me. I'm learning!

My undying devotion goes to Michael Cowan for giving me my first HUGE break at the *Today* show.

Many thanks to Sheila O'Shea for believing in this project and passing it on to George Andreou.

To George Andreou, the best editor in the world, who by this time could be a fabulous dog trainer.

I can't leave out my golden retriever Opal, who is the why in all of this.

And finally, to my students, past and present, whose dogs taught me everything I know. I'm glad I listened because they had a lot to say!

Thank you to the following dogs, who so generously volunteered to be in the pictures:

Daisy "star of stage and screen" Granoff, the former wild-child puppy, now referred to as the model of good manners for all goldendoodles, which is a golden retriever crossed with a poodle. Really. Would I kid you?

Face Santo, my son's dog, who used to be a Jack Russell and is now a Parson Russell terrier. Go figure.

Quick Santo, my Border collie from Wildfire kennels (Pat Schulz) in Lake Forest, Illinois. This dog owns my heart.

Cheddar Santo, my daughter's manic Border collie, another Wildfire dog—the best!

Quigley Morton, a labradoodle (Labrador/poodle mix) whose motto, which *used* to be "What can I do *to* you?", is now "What can I do *for* you?!" See, all the training paid off!

Kobe Creamer, the world's sexiest Doberman. 'Nuff said.

Flik Osborne, Heidi's Border collie (from Wildfire, of course!), who we now know, after all the time we spent taking and retaking the pictures, is the most patient creature on God's green earth!

Cyle Boland, the super-adorable Cavalier King Charles spaniel. Yes, he's real!!!

Abbey Boland, a yellow Labrador retriever who personifies the phrase "What can I do for you?"

Amelia Bedilia, the Maltese. I know, she's sooooooo cute!!

Biscuit Kloorfain, a golden retriever who's always willing to please . . . after lots of obedience training, right, Mike?

Gracie Peck-Thompson, a sweet, placid labradoodle. Stop laughing, Betty! This dog is so famous that she had to hyphenate her last name when she got married.

Ebony Togher, a cocker spaniel, who spends most of the summer at my house. One minute she was lounging around the pool, the next she was in front of the camera. "But, Mr. DeMille, wait a minute, I'm not ready for my close-up!"

Sami Davidowitz, the Shiba Inu, a lovely Japanese dog whose name translates to mean "Little . . ."—never mind. Ask Debby.

Buddy Formento, a multicultural dog who is unbelievably sweet. Animal shelters are filled with wonderful dogs like Buddy!

Rosie Kourgalis—a Labrador retriever. That's it. No poodle, no doodle, just a Lab. Her sweetness is matched only by that of her owner, Caryl.

Sandy Steiger—a soft-coated wheaton terrier. Sure, she shredded some valuable family heirloom pictures, but that was when she was a puppy! Now she's the poster child for Well-Behaved Wheatons.

Bailey "BE QUIET!!!!" Maher—a West Highland white terrier. Obedient? Yes. Pavarotti? Not even close.

Mocha(chino) Pendana, another multicultural dog. She's the dog with me in the book jacket picture, she's on my business cards, she's on my website, and she's also in my heart! Her motto is "Will work for tennis balls!" I still owe her a few cases!

And last but not least, thank you to the human in the pictures: *Heidi Osborne,* who is such a good friend that she even took her soft cast off her broken wrist to re-do some of the shots. We Photoshopped out her grimaces of pain. Just kidding!

INDEX

(Page references in *italic* refer to illustrations.)

A Note About the Author

Kathy Santo has trained dogs for both home and competition. She currently sees more than 100 dogs each week at her obedience school and offers advice to hundreds of owners through her seminars and camps. She lives in New Jersey with her husband, two children, and three dogs.

A Note on the Type

The text of this book was composed in Apollo, the first typeface ever originated specifically for film composition. Designed by Adrian Frutiger and issued by the Monotype Corporation of London in 1964, Apollo is not only a versatile typeface suitable for many uses but also pleasant to read in all of its sizes.

Composed by North Market Street Graphics,
Lancaster, Pennsylvania
Printed and bound by R. R. Donnelley & Sons,
Harrisonburg, Virginia
Paw prints by Kato Olsson
Designed by Virginia Tan